Abundance to Zen

Wisdom for a Fulfilling Life

Paul Hudon

HIGHER SELF
PUBLISHING

A Higher Self Publication
Higher Self Publishing Registered Offices: Elgin, Arizona 85611

2024 Paul Hudon

Paperback ISBN: 978-1-7357669-1-1

Digital ISBN: 978-1-7357669-2-8

Author Paul Hudon
Abundance to Zen: Wisdom for a Fulfilling Life

Published in the United States of America

Cover Design and Interior Graphics: Elisa Tanaka
Digital version produced by BookNook.Biz

While the author made every effort to provide accurate information at the time of publication, neither the publisher nor the author assumes any responsibility for errors, or for changes that may occur after publication.

This book is creative nonfiction. The information and events in this book are the experiences and ideas of the author. The ideas in this book have been expressed and written as remembered by the author.

For more information on how to purchase this book or to schedule the author for speaking engagements, please contact the author directly at paulhudonauthor@gmail.com.

I'm fortunate to have traveled around the sun as many times as I have with my lovely wife Jane.

Over the course of each trip, we encourage each other to uncover a part of ourselves we never knew existed.

This allows us the freedom to recreate ourselves with the intention of living to the fullness of who we are meant to be.

To say I'm lucky to have such a supportive partner on this journey is an understatement.

It is with much love and respect I dedicate this book to her.

Table of Contents

E

F

G

H

I

J

K

L

M

N

T

U

V

W

X

Y

Z

Preface

AT AN EARLY AGE WE ARE taught the alphabet. From those lessons we learn to read, write, and express ourselves. It's amazing what we can accomplish when we master those twenty-six letters.

Individually, letters have little strength, but when we link them together with other letters we can create great works of literature, powerful speeches, and of course, words of love and compassion. Yet sadly, the opposite is also true.

I never really considered the power of words until I began to write. I realized a simple series of words could change the direction of a person's life, mine included. How often do we stop to hear the words we speak? Do we understand the force behind these words?

As I wrote *A-Z* I had to consider many words that had the potential to raise an eyebrow or question my motives. Yet as you read through the chapters, if a subject surprises you, that's good, read on. Oftentimes we need to hear a message differently to have it truly settle into our consciousness.

I thought writing *A-Z* would be fun, although I knew it would have its challenges. I wanted to write something different, yet relevant, something that would cause us to think, while not being too heavy or overbearing.

With most of the chapters, finding the right titles was easy, although at times there were too many options. Then there were the chapters where it was a bit more challenging; "X" and "Z" come to mind. An internet search helped solve that problem.

Sitting at my desk thinking about writing this type of book, I recall my younger self, struggling to spell, pronounce, and read the simplest of stories. Thankfully, it didn't stop me from recognizing that the world was available to me when I held an open book in my hands. All because of the way we organize groups of letters from the twenty-six we are given.

I must admit, at times I still struggle with spelling. Although I have gotten much better, I often revert to pronouncing unfamiliar words phonetically. All this means is that no matter what obstacles are placed in front of us, if we want to succeed, we can overcome just about anything.

I hope you enjoy reading *A-Z.* You might come up with a few titles I missed. If so, in a journal, write that chapter for yourself. See how it goes, what lessons will you uncover? Don't be shy, the journey begins when we link a few letters together.

Introduction

THE IDEA FOR THIS BOOK CAME to me loud and clear one afternoon when I was searching for a theme. I heard, "Write the alphabet." From there, things began to fall into place. Each letter of the alphabet would be a chapter title, with four mini chapters based on different subjects beginning with the same letter as the main chapter, B has Balance and Blame, L has Limitations and Love, for example.

I chose the subjects according to how they made me feel. Was there a message I could create from the title? I thought it might be easier to remember the lessons each chapter held if it could be associated with a letter.

As a writer, I'm always trying to simplify my message, then introducing it into mainstream thinking. If it's too complicated we walk away, thereby denying ourselves a chance at the best life possible.

Yet if I can present a self-help idea in a language that does not make us squeamish, then I consider myself a success. Who doesn't want to learn more about regret, monsters, or showing up for ourselves? Are we resilient when challenges arise?

One of the pillars of this book, as with all my writing, is love. I see no point in writing anything that diminishes the value of others. Can we love those who are different than we are, even though they may hate us? Is it possible to love ourselves no matter what others think?

My intention is for you to reconnect with your own power-ful self-love. I use the word "reconnect" for a reason. I believe we were all born into our physical body knowing this love, but during the course of life we have lost touch with this eternal source of compassion.

Please read this book anyway you like, A to Z, Z to A, or start with the letters of your first name, it's your choice. A side effect of reading *A-Z* might be that you begin to feel the fire of your authentic self burning brighter with each chapter you read.

My hat is off to you for having the inspiration to pick up this book and begin the journey of living your best life – from A to Z.

Abundance

When we look closely at our lives, do we have a clear understanding of the abundance surrounding us? Or do we have a perception of lack? If we measure the material things we possess, are we really seeing abundance, or are we just noticing the stuff we have accumulated? Things wear out, get lost, and we may lose interest in them. Possessions that once had meaning can soon become memories that can weigh us down emotionally.

If we were to turn our gaze within and search for the richness found in our lives, we might begin to understand the meaning of abundance. Yet we must be willing to take an honest journey, otherwise our thoughts of lack will derail any truth we discover.

One of the lessons I have learned along my spiritual journey is the abundance of love flowing through my heart, and the hearts of all people. I wasn't always aware of this love. Only when I began the search for a deeper connection in my life did I discover this eternal source of love.

This is not a love of material objects, power, or money, but a true abundance of authentic, unconditional love for me and everyone on the planet. Yet we may question why we do not feel or experience this love more often. One of the many reasons is because we think this love does not exist. Or we could have experienced great emotional pain and as a result we have built walls around our heart for protection. We don't realize these walls also prevent love from flowing into our lives.

Another reason we may not feel very abundant is because we are searching for love in the wrong places. By looking to others for love we will limit the way we experience love. If we try to connect with someone who is not aware of the abundance of love within themselves, we will be asking them to love us in a way they cannot. We are seeking their love as a way to feel whole and complete, yet to feel whole and complete we must first love ourselves.

This is why we must begin to explore what is true and right for us. It is on this journey where we begin to sift through the things that have meaning for us and discard those that do not, from our awareness. Some of these things may be physical objects, while others may be thoughts and beliefs that no longer serve our highest good.

If we are holding onto anger from years past, we may be hindering our ability to experience love now, because our anger will get in the way. Yet if we learn to forgive, and let go of what no longer serves us, we will start to feel an abundance of our own love circulating within our being.

As our awareness of love begins to flow, we will notice more reasons to love. We will have replaced our negative mental chatter with love, our judgement with love, and our need for the approval of others with our loving approval of ourselves.

Through this realization, we learn to share our abundance of love with others without conditions or expectations. If our love is true and authentic, we will not be asking for love in return for the love we give. We can give love freely without the expectation of love as a reward.

Our view on abundance will all come down to how we see

the world. If we feel the world owes us something, we will always have the feeling of lack, because we have not received what we want. This will only cause us to want more because we will never have enough.

When we learn that true abundance originates within us, we will never lack for one of the most important things needed for a true and authentic life, an abundance of love.

Accountability

W<small>HEN WE LOOK IN THE MIRROR,</small> do we see a person who is accountable for their behavior? Or do we see someone who blames others for the way life has turned out? If our intention is to live a truthful and authentic life, we must learn to be accountable for our actions.

It's never easy to accept responsibility for our actions, especially if our actions cause others pain. We may blame them for their behavior, believing they provoked us into acting as we did. Yet this is not a loving way to live. Our reasons to blame becomes a wall we think protects us from having to be accountable for our actions. We fail to realize these walls prevent us from experiencing the fullness of life.

One of the challenges we face with being accountable for our behavior is having to accept how our life is unfolding. Accountability means we have no one to blame for the life we are living. This seems harsh because life can challenge us in many ways, although we are responsible for how we react to these challenges.

It may be easy to say the dog ate my assignment, or it's their fault, assuming we are free and clear of any responsibility, yet this is not always the case. Being accountable is accepting the role we play in our successes and failures, as well as in our emotional highs and lows. Sure, life can throw us a curveball every once in a while, but in these situations there will be important lessons meant for our emotional growth.

I remember having an uncomfortable intuitive feeling about an upcoming motorcycle ride. I ignored the feeling and went on the ride anyway. After getting injured, I realized I would have been better off staying home. I could have blamed the pace of the ride, or the unfamiliar terrain, but my health and well-being are my responsibility.

Throughout the healing process I had to hold myself accountable for the outcome. No one in the group was controlling the throttle on my motorcycle, but me. The lessons I learned from this experience were painful in many ways, although I now recognize the importance of an uncomfortable intuitive feeling.

Not only in the physical world must we be accountable. Our emotional world also needs accountability. We may hear unkind words from those around us, but do we have to absorb these words into our awareness? When we realize we have a choice in how we react to others, we can choose to remain centered and ignore what others say. Thereby choosing instead to maintain a calm state of mind, rather than reacting out of anger.

Emotional accountability asks the question, "How are we supporting ourselves?" Meaning, are we giving ourselves the best opportunities to succeed, and the best chances to fulfill our dreams and passions? When we accept responsibility for our thoughts, words, and actions, we recognize that the outcome of our life choices will be determined by how accountable we are to ourselves.

No matter how challenging a situation may be, how we conduct ourselves will reveal to us if we have taken responsibility for the way we handle the struggles we often face in life. Knowing it is important to be accountable to ourselves will remind us that the life we are living, and the life we want to live, are our responsibility. Being accountable for our thoughts, words, and actions, gives us the best chance to live to the fullness of who we are.

Associates

THERE'S A SAYING THAT GOES, "WE are judged by those with whom we associate." Although we may disagree, there is much truth in those words. If we examine our friendships closely, we will notice how these relationships influence the trajectory of our lives.

At first glance, being judged by the company we keep may not seem like much, yet are these associates encouraging us to live to the fullness of who we are? Or are they doing what they can to keep us close to them, thereby preventing us from realizing our full potential?

If we intend to live an authentic life, we must associate with people who support us while not being afraid of us leaving them if our paths diverge. Yet we must be willing to do the same if their journey takes them away from us.

It can be difficult to accept that not all the people in our life will be with us each and every day. Our life is in a constant state of flux, no matter how much we try to resist change, change will happen. Because of this, our associates will change as well.

I remember a time when I realized my associates were not supportive of my journey. It wasn't easy, but I understood that to live a healthier life, I needed to make a change. In doing so, my circle of friends was rearranged, improving the quality of my life.

Our associates are often a place of comfort. We connect with them when we are struggling, as well as when we celebrate our victories. This is why moving away from those who do not align with our truth may seem difficult. We know them, even though they may not be the best for our emotional health, we work to convince ourselves that being with them is better than being alone.

The fear of searching for new associates may keep us from living a life that has true meaning. Yet if we want supporters who will help us elevate our consciousness, we must connect with people who will challenge us to shift our mindset.

We cannot expect to live a life that exceeds our expectations if we continue our old, unhealthy patterns of thought and behavior. This can be difficult because we need to clear away the thoughts and beliefs that limit our emotional growth.

One way to accomplish this is to ask if a thought, or belief, is powered by positive energy. If so, then this thought or belief benefits us emotionally. If not, we have to ask ourselves why we are carrying this negative energy within our consciousness.

This is where difficulty may arise. By changing our thoughts and beliefs we may lose touch with those who once called us a friend. But are we here on Earth to make ourselves small as a way to make others comfortable?

When we begin the journey of discovering our authentic self, we open many doors that at one time were closed. Once we cross the threshold of a fresh opportunity, new people will enter our lives.

These new associates will share a similar mindset. Although we may not agree on everything, their point of view may give us the chance to see the world from a different perspective. Any disagreement will not develop into a war of words but create an opening into other possibilities we have not considered.

There may be occasions when we do not have close confidants or trusted friends. This might be a time of difficulty, although it can also be an opportunity for self-discovery, something we could not experience if we were surrounded by people and their opinions.

To live an authentic life, we must be honest with ourselves and those around us. If we cannot live truthfully, it might be time to find new associates. Otherwise, we may never realize the truth of who we are.

Authenticity

IN THE WORLD TODAY, IT CAN be challenging to be authentic. There is constant pressure to be someone who "fits in" rather than being our authentic self. Yet isn't the person we truly are the one we want to show to the world? What is the point of being anything other than our authentic self?

We all have a desire to be liked and admired by others, but if our goal is to "fit in" will we change who we are to be accepted? Each of us is unique, yet isn't our uniqueness what makes us stand out from the crowd?

From the time we were born until today we have had many opportunities to please those in our lives. None of us want to disappoint others, so we will do whatever it takes to maintain their favorable opinion of us, even if we have to change who we are. This is where we lose our authenticity.

The challenge begins when we realize that who we truly are is overshadowed by the false façade we create by fitting in. The person who is at the core of our being is hidden beneath the never-ending work of pleasing others. Yet how long can we live this way, and will we ever be truly happy living behind a false front?

How do we recognize if we are not living by our authenticity? The answer is rather simple, do we love ourselves, and are we sharing this love with others? This is not a narcissistic-driven love, but a true, deep love that places no limitations, conditions, or expectations on who we, or others, are.

Once we realize the answer is to love ourselves, we must begin to live by this love. This means to strive to live to the fullness of who we are. A love as strong and deep as this allows us the courage to experience life in new and powerful ways. It is in this loving place where we don't hold back. We give ourselves the best opportunity to succeed at whatever makes our heart and soul sing for joy.

Within this love is the courage we need to question our beliefs, and discard those that do not support our authentic self. We can then step away from the limited version of who we think we are. This gives us the chance to express our truth to the world without the fear of upsetting those we love. Their behavior toward our authenticity reflects who they are, and the limiting beliefs they may hold within themselves.

The thing about discovering the love that is at the foundation of our authentic self, is we now love our uniqueness. We are not ashamed to show the world who we are. Rather than change to make others happy, we can cultivate our own dreams and true desires, based on an honest feeling of what makes us authentic. It is here where the façade we have been maintaining begins to crumble and fall away, revealing our true selves to the world.

As we become familiar with our authenticity, we realize we can encourage others to find their inner truth as well. We will no longer ask others to play it small for us. We want to experience the fullness of who they are, hear their authentic voices, and witness the rebirth of their uniqueness. This is what unconditional love is all about, seeing people for who they truly are.

Each one of us has an authentic self. We may be living it now, or it may be hidden. Yet to live a truthful, authentic, self-loving life, we must be willing to break free from a version of ourselves that is limited and outdated.

B

Balance

THERE IS MUCH WE CAN CONTROL in life, and much we cannot. Somewhere between the two is a place of balance. When we realize the outcome of any challenging situation will depend on how we react, we will have the insight to remain balanced. It is in this place where we are the most connected to the inner guidance needed to benefit us the most.

Balance is a funny thing, one minute we are centered, and all is well, the next minute we fall flat on our face. The interesting thing about being in balance is we may be constantly shifting from one mindset to another.

The choices we make when life gets tough will determine whether we remain balanced or not. How often do we react to negativity without much thought? In doing so, the experience controls us and throws us off center. From there it can take a while to regain our balance.

When we accept that we can control our reactions to negative situations, we have the ability to remain in balance throughout the experience. When our state of balance is important to us, choosing the self-loving solution will be the most beneficial for our well-being. Think of it as loving ourselves so much, we would rather remain in balance than allow any negative emotions to overtake us.

As with trying to balance ourselves on one foot with our arms outstretched, we know being in balance takes practice.

With an awareness of the importance of being balanced emotionally, we realize we do not have to become involved in the issues that once brought stress into our lives.

One of the things I've noticed when in a balanced state of being, is I can see the solutions to the problems at hand clearly. While in balance, my mind is free from all the clutter that can cause a lack of emotional harmony. I have learned that being in balance clears my mind.

How do we reach a place of true balance? One way is to courageously challenge many of the thoughts and beliefs we repeat to ourselves throughout the day. If a thought or belief is not founded on love it is worth discarding from our awareness. Why do we think thoughts not rooted in love? Because we never understood how much these thoughts dictate our attitude and control the outcome of our life.

When we begin the work of questioning our thoughts and beliefs, we quickly see how many of these thoughts are not worth our attention. Remember, our thoughts and beliefs create our words and actions. If we have a hard time focusing on our thoughts, and beliefs, listen to the words we speak, and the actions we take. This will be a telltale sign if we are living a balanced life or not.

As we continue to discard unnecessary thoughts and beliefs, our consciousness begins to fill with thoughts and beliefs that will truly benefit our life. These thoughts and beliefs are much healthier for us physically, emotionally, and spiritually. It is in this place where we begin to mature as a person.

While working to release thoughts and beliefs that do not serve our higher good, we become a place of comfort for those in our life. They know they can count on us to remain clear-headed when challenges arise. In this way, our place of balance contributes to the overall well-being of others, allowing us to control that which at one time, controlled us.

Blame

BLAME IS AN EMOTION THAT CAN easily trap us in the grip of negativity. It doesn't take much thought to blame others. Oftentimes blame shifts our responsibility for our well-being away from where it belongs. It also strengthens our anger. When we choose blame, we are taking the easy way out.

There are situations that are out of our control, but the way we react to these events is our responsibility. If we choose to blame, and it IS a choice, we are allowing the negative situation to overtake us emotionally. We may say it was someone else's fault, the circumstances weren't right, or we got caught up in the group energy and lost our emotional center, so we chose to blame others for the outcome.

There are reasons why we blame. One is because we do not want to accept responsibility for our actions. When we look at our ability to heal from a painful emotional or physical experience, we must be willing to take responsibility for our healing. This can be a challenge because the reason we often blame is because we lack an honest understanding of the healing energy found in our true self-love.

This powerful source of love gives us the strength and courage to be accountable for our actions. Yet because of the depth of this love, we can forgive ourselves and possibly those who have caused our pain. Self-love also helps us move forward, leaving the painful memory behind.

If we continue to blame, we carry the weight of this negative energy into the present moment, thereby impacting the way we experience life. Although our blame may give us a sense of entitlement and righteousness, it truly serves us no good.

It's easy to recognize that the foundation of blame is anger. We cannot heal when we are focused on anything rooted in negative energy. If we constantly blame, we are reactivating this negativity in our consciousness. This is similar to poking a physical wound we wish would heal. Each time we touch the injury we delay our healing.

Blame harms us emotionally because we create a false persona founded on our reasons to blame. The more we speak of these reasons, the more our persona grows in strength. This is unhealthy for us and for those we love.

If we use blame to justify our false persona, then this persona will impact the way we experience our authentic self. The question may arise, "If I heal, what then, who am I?" Where does that leave our persona, or our self-righteous anger? It may be more comfortable for us to remain in a state of blame than to challenge our wounded identity and move toward healing.

When we seek to recover from a painful experience, we must realize that to truly love ourselves we must be willing to set aside the reasons we choose to blame. Once we begin the healing process, the persona we built on negativity starts to lose its grip on our lives, allowing love to take over. Love gives us the strength to release our need to blame, because we understand it is healthier to have the energy of love flowing through our life.

The interesting thing about life is we always have a choice. We can choose the negativity of blame, or the love of forgiveness. Either way the outcome of our life will be shaped by this choice.

Choosing love may not be easy, but love will always make life better than if we chose to blame. The next time we think of blaming others, we can take responsibility for our emotional health and seek the loving alternative.

Blessings

IT CAN BE EASY FOCUSING ON the challenges we have experienced in life. We often share these difficulties as a way to get attention and sympathy from others. Then we use their empathy as a means to boost our self-esteem. Thereby encouraging us to continue with this line of behavior.

What if instead of valuing ourselves through adversity, we chose to appreciate and share our blessings? Think of all the things that have helped us along our journey. Wouldn't this elevate our consciousness to a state of gratitude?

This seems all well and good, but one reason we rarely share our blessings is because we will be seen as bragging about the good that has entered our lives. In doing so we may lose the support of our friends. Many times they would rather wallow with us in our struggles than support us in our blessings.

It may seem odd we are uncomfortable sharing the wonderful things happening in our lives. Is it because we believe others would feel threatened by our success? We all experience blessings, yet we often keep them to ourselves because we don't want those around us to feel awkward.

This behavior is rooted in the belief that if someone achieves a goal or milestone, they have taken something away from others. There is no truth in this belief. If we receive a blessing in the form of an opportunity, it does not take anything away from others. Every one of us experiences blessings in life if we are aware enough to recognize them.

We don't always have to share our blessings with those around us. If we notice that telling others about our blessings bothers them, we can keep them to ourselves. There is no harm in holding our blessings close to our heart until the time is right to share them.

A powerful lesson about blessings is the more we express gratitude for them, the more blessings we will experience. Gratitude acts like a magnet attracting back to us more reasons to be grateful. Remember, being grateful for our blessings is a great way to receive more blessings.

Our blessings will come in many different shapes. They may arrive as a fuzzy puppy, a beautiful day for a family gathering, the perfect life partner. Even a rain shower can be seen as a blessing. It will all depend on our state of mind.

If we are living in alignment with our authentic self, we will recognize blessings everywhere we look. Yes, there will be times when we aren't open to seeing the blessings surrounding us. The best way to change this is to search for small blessings, then add another, and another.

When times are difficult, and we would like to shift our mindset, we could make a list of our blessings. At first we may only find a few, but if we take an honest look at our life, we may notice more and more blessings. The intention is to create a list of blessings, giving us an opportunity to reflect on how fortunate we truly are.

With each passing day we have a choice, recognize our blessings, or go through the day thinking about how difficult life can be. Yet if we are on the path to living an authentic life, we will notice the blessings in every challenge we face.

Boundaries

THE WORLD IS AN INTERESTING PLACE. We are living together on this planet separated by boundaries. Some are real, like oceans, rivers, walls, and languages. Others we place around ourselves as a form of protection. Some boundaries benefit us, while others hinder our ability to see those we share this planet with clearly.

There is a saying that people need healthy boundaries to go through life. But how do we establish boundaries without upsetting those we love, or alienating those we want in our lives?

One reason people create boundaries is because they want to maintain their "space," a place of serenity and peace. This "space" is often needed when it comes to those who can be toxic or hostile. However, this "space" can increase the distance between us and those who are concerned with our well-being.

Boundaries can be advantageous to us when we need a break from the hectic world. Finding time for our well-being requires boundaries. We are so connected to the outside world; we often forget to give ourselves a much-needed rest from the constant barrage of information. It is here where boundaries are helpful.

It's also possible our boundaries are suppressing our emotional and spiritual growth. Could our boundaries be founded on fear? Or do these boundaries limit the way we experience the world? Here is an example. To truly love, we must be willing to step outside of our boundaries and expose a part of ourselves our boundaries once protected. This can be a place of great vulnerability. Our choices may limit the depth of love we experience.

Boundaries are different than the walls we often build to protect our wounded heart. We create boundaries for many of the same reasons we build walls, although we may be more flexible emotionally with our boundaries. This flexibility allows us to remain open to give and receive love, but strong enough to keep others at arms-length if needed.

If we are preventing love from entering our life for fear of being hurt emotionally, then we have isolated ourselves from the outside world because of the walls we have built. It may take an honest self-examination to know if we have boundaries, or walls surrounding us.

How would we know if we have built walls, or if we have healthy boundaries? Walls originate from past emotional or physical pain. They have been built as defense mechanisms keeping everything out, but walls also keep the pain in. If we have not healed from a painful experience, then we have built walls. Boundaries allow us the space to heal while recognizing the lessons painful experiences have taught us.

By establishing healthy boundaries, we create a situation where the wisdom of our inner voice will be heard. This loving source of guidance helps us understand if we need to keep people at a distance or welcome them into our lives.

Boundaries also give us the strength to make our emotional health a priority. We can set aside time for anything that brings us a sense of inner peace, while not feeling guilty in the process.

We may believe that boundaries are limitations, hindering our ability to live by our inner truth, this is not the case. Imagine healthy boundaries as guidelines leading us toward what is true and right for us. Once we understand that our boundaries keep us on course, we realize they do not block our ability to live to the fullness of who we are.

C

Character

JOHANN WOLFGANG VON GOETHE SAID, "YOU can easily judge the character of a man by how he treats those who can do nothing for him." Much to consider in this simple yet powerful sentence. This quote may cause us to self-reflect and examine our own behavior.

How do we treat those who can do nothing for us? Are we compassionate to those who appear homeless? Do we see those less fortunate than us as not being worth our consideration? These questions may seem easy to answer, but are we being honest with ourselves?

This can be a complicated subject because the way we treat others may have been taught to us by those who claim to love us. We believe our actions are justified because our beliefs tell us so. Yet what would happen if we took an honest look in the mirror as we were interacting with others? Would we be pleased with our behavior?

The interesting thing about life is that at any moment our life could change. One moment we could be on top of the world with all our wants and needs available to us, the next, we might be working an unfulfilling job, or struggling to find a warm place to sleep. When we truly understand this, we begin to realize that those who can do nothing for us may have faced struggles we know nothing about.

A powerful lesson I have learned along my spiritual journey is that everyone is doing the best they can. This can be difficult to accept because we often judge others based on the standards we set for ourselves. In other words, we want others to act in a way that matches our beliefs and values.

This makes us comfortable because many times we judge others to boost our fragile self-esteem. If we treat those who can do nothing for us poorly, we have already judged them and have condemned them to our scorn. As if our scorn has value outside of our own sphere of judgement.

In truth, how we treat others is a reflection of who we are. This thought can make us uncomfortable and if it does, then good! It forces us to take an honest look at our thoughts and beliefs to uncover why we are behaving this way.

Our beliefs have been created by the thoughts we think, and the lessons we have learned throughout life. If we have been taught that those who can do nothing for us are not worth our time, then we will create a belief system that supports these thoughts.

We must learn to understand that our thoughts and beliefs create our life experiences. What we believe, we will see in the world, reinforcing our beliefs. If we believe small dogs are vicious, then every small dog we encounter is a perceived threat. The same type of belief will hold true for people as well.

Another powerful lesson I have learned, is we all originated from the same source of energy. This energy is eternal, unconditional love. Hard to imagine because at times we are not a very loving people. We love those who agree with us and choose to fight those who do not.

Finding common ground becomes challenging because we are too attached to our judgement of others. Our thoughts and beliefs now control the way we see and interact with the world around us. In a way, we cannot see past our beliefs because we use them as a wall protecting us from anything that does not align with what we believe.

In living this way, we limit the possibilities available to us. We only see what we want to see and cannot see anything else. Here is where our character is developed, forming our behavior toward others. We lack awareness of the love at the core of our being, and we fail to recognize and accept that everyone is doing the best they can.

Little do we know how our beliefs and behavior separates us from our true self, and the life that is possible when we live by the love at the center of who we are. If we were to break down the walls of our limiting beliefs, we might begin to see the world through the eyes of the eternal love of our creation. We would then realize that we are all one people and our behavior toward others does indeed matter.

Any work needed to return to a place of loving consciousness begins with examining how we treat those who can do nothing for us. It is along this path where we will recognize the truth of our character.

Compass

I REMEMBER MY FATHER TEACHING ME to use a compass to guide the way. I was fascinated by how the magnetic pull would always turn the needle toward north. He showed me which direction I was traveling, and how to retrace my steps if needed.

Oftentimes in life, a compass would be a beneficial guide leading us through the challenges we face. In the physical world this is easy to understand. Yet in our inner, emotional world, a compass may not serve a useful purpose.

This is where our intuition, instincts, and gut feelings come into play. What if we were to accept that these powerful feelings are our inner compass? Is it possible to be guided through life by the subtle feelings we receive from our intuition or gut feelings?

It took me a few years to trust using a compass in the wilderness. I remember a hike in Southern Utah where it was essential to take a compass bearing on a distant butte, before dropping into a canyon with limited points of reference. From then on, we traveled by this bearing. This required a lot of trust in the compass, because to travel in the canyon safely, we had to maintain the bearing accurately.

The same is true for our intuitive feelings, we need to learn to trust them even when we cannot see the path forward clearly. The thing about intuition is we may never know the reasons for an uncomfortable gut feeling if we change plans to ease the discomfort. But we will always know if our choice to disregard the intuitive guidance was the right decision.

Think of ignoring our intuition as taking a compass bearing on our destination, then tossing the compass aside. We have valuable information in our hands, but we choose to ignore this information. If we find ourselves lost, we only have to look at our own actions to understand why.

Intuition works in similar ways. No matter which direction we choose, we will always have an intuitive feeling guiding the way. It is our responsibility to ourselves to pay attention to this guidance, then make the safe and healthy choices. The outcome of the experience will reveal to us if we have followed the guidance or not.

There are times when a compass can't be trusted. The compass points to magnetic north, although when around metal objects the needle may veer off course. The same thing can happen when we are in situations that challenge us emotionally. It can be a struggle to know what is true and right for us when we are around people who cause us to doubt ourselves.

The best way to resolve this is to find time to move to a quiet place to allow ourselves the opportunity to focus on our intuition, and the guidance it speaks. This gives us a chance to recognize what resonates deep within us. Just as the compass needle needs to settle before it can be trusted, so, too, do our emotions and instincts.

When we trust our intuitive feelings as guidance, we will have access to a compass leading us through life's challenges. All we have to do is learn to trust the information we receive.

Confidence

CONFIDENCE CAN BE AN INTERESTING STATE of being. When we think of those who are confident, are they boastful, or do they brag about themselves? How often have we encountered people who are always talking about themselves, without concern for what others are thinking or feeling? But is this the true meaning of confidence? Shouldn't confidence be humble?

Many years ago I met a man who had every right to brag about his accomplishments. What I noticed about him was when he was with a group of people, he showed more interest in what others were doing than he did in talking about himself. If asked about his achievements, he would talk for a bit, then shift the conversation to a more inclusive topic.

I admired him for his ability to create a group discussion rather than a one-sided narrative. This man was confident with who he was. He did not need the admiration of others to boost his self-esteem. It was a pleasure to be with him because he was interested in what other people were experiencing.

Confidence comes from a deeply rooted trust in who a person is. They know themselves well enough that they do not need to draw attention to themselves to make themselves feel valued. They also love themselves enough to be humble and low key.

How do we reach such an emotional state? Confidence begins with knowing that within every challenging situation there will be important lessons meant for our emotional growth. Even if we fail, there will be lessons within the experience that will help us gain confidence.

Another key component of confidence is self-love. When we love ourselves, we know we are always doing the best we can in any given situation. If we knew more, we would be doing our best as well. Our self-love gives us the strength to recognize there is no need for the self-defeating behavior of self-doubt, bragging, or putting others down as a way to make ourselves feel better.

When a challenging situation arises, we do our best, learn what we can, then move forward with this new wisdom. If we are confident there is no reason to agonize over our behavior. We understand we did what we could, as best as possible, and we move on growing from the experience. This gives us the courage to see ourselves as someone who is in a constant state of learning. Whether we succeed or not, we are always improving from the challenges we face.

As we reach a place of confidence, we also create inner peace. The mental chatter that often distracts us is now silenced because our self-love is our underlying state of being. We love ourselves enough to know which of our thoughts need our attention, and which we can ignore. We also know that the behavior of others is a reflection of what they are going through emotionally.

Confidence allows us to choose the loving path when it comes to the way others are acting. When we are confident, we have no need to become emotionally involved in the drama others often thrive on.

At times our confidence will be challenged, as the world can shift quickly, catching us off guard. Although if we are stable in our confidence beforehand, we will quickly return to a balanced emotional state of mind.

The foundation of true confidence is self-love. It is this love that prevents us from treating others poorly. We see no reason to put others down because we know they are learning from their challenges just as we are.

Arriving at a state of confidence, we share our lives with others without the need for their validation or the expectation of their approval. This allows us the humility needed to listen to what others are saying without judgement.

True confidence is seeing everyone through the eyes of our self-love and knowing that gaining confidence begins with loving ourselves.

Contemplation

Each of us needs a few moments of contemplation throughout our day. Even though we feel we are too busy to find time to observe and reflect, this time will benefit us greatly. How often have we caught ourselves staring off in the distance, with no real thoughts? We may think this time is wasted, but this is not the case.

Occasionally I believe being in a state of contemplation is more beneficial than my time in meditation. As I look out the window, I may follow a bird flying through the gardens. Or watch a bee float from one flower to another. I'm observing the world around me, which silences the inner world screaming for my attention, something I struggle with in meditation.

Think of contemplation as allowing our thoughts to drift past without becoming involved with them. When my mind is busy during meditation, I let my thoughts sail by without my involvement, like watching clouds move across the sky.

Contemplation gives us the space to see what thoughts and ideas are hidden beneath all the other thoughts we think are priorities. In a way, contemplation is an act of not thinking about our thoughts, although we know they are there.

The challenge with taking time for contemplation is we have been taught to be productive, and if we are staring out the window, we are wasting time. These powerful false beliefs can be difficult to overcome in our success-driven world.

Yet contemplation is a gateway to finding clarity in a thought-crowded world. It is here where we are not too focused but are in a state of allowing guidance to flow to us. How often have you come across a solution to a problem when you weren't thinking about it? This is one of the benefits of contemplation.

In a way, finding the time to contemplate requires inner strength. The inner chatter is often amplified when we are sitting idly, watching the waves wash the beach, or the shadows of clouds move across the landscape. Do we become guilt-ridden when we silence the chatter, to quietly observe the beauty around us?

As a writer, I have noticed that future writing topics come to mind easier when I'm in contemplation, rather than when I'm actively seeking a topic. It's much like finding your lost car keys when you're not looking for them.

We may believe we must always be doing something. Is this mindset productive? What about taking care of our emotional health? Isn't that important as well? I believe contemplation is a non-action, action. We are taking steps to improve our state of mind, even though we appear to be doing nothing physically.

With easy access to the world at our fingertips, we have become addicted to being in touch with all that is going on around us. It's as if the world has come to live with us, and we don't know how to put an end to our relationship.

Yet we can do little for much of what we see happening around us. Although one thing we can do is to find our place of emotional center. It is here where we can use the wisdom found in contemplation to benefit ourselves, and the lives of those we share our life with.

Contemplation does not require any special training. It is

an act of self-love we can practice anywhere. Rather than get caught up in the hustle and bustle of life, in contemplation we can allow life to move past, like a cloud we can't touch as we watch its shadow drift across the landscape.

D

Detachment

FROM AN EARLY AGE, WE HAVE been taught to seek approval from those around us. Through this process, we have learned that if someone likes us, we have value. If a person loves us, we love ourselves. In this way we attach our happiness and well-being to the reactions of others.

This can be a tricky way to live because our emotional state of being is connected to whether people like, accept, or love us. When we live this way, our self-image and self-worth balance on the behavior of others. If they are upset or are too focused on something they are dealing with to give us the emotional support we need, we may think they don't love us. If, and when, this happens, our world comes crashing down. It's only when we feel accepted by them again that we regain our self-worth.

In situations like these, we may feel as if we are on an emotional rollercoaster. One moment we are high because others are showing an interest in our life, then the next, we are plummeting to the bottom because they may not have time for us. In a sense the behavior of others controls us emotionally. By living this way, every aspect of our life will be affected.

As we take a closer look as to why we live this way, we may notice the root cause of our behavior is because we look to others for acceptance and validation. We are handing this responsibility to others because we have not accepted this responsibility for ourselves.

Yet, the deeper cause of our behavior is a lack of self-love. As challenging as this may appear, when we truly love ourselves, we do not need the support of those in our life to boost our self-worth. In other words, we love ourselves enough to maintain our emotional balance no matter what others say or do.

There is tremendous strength in our self-love. It is in this strength we find the courage to detach ourselves from our need for outside validation, or approval. Even though we may still seek acceptance from those around us, our emotional health and happiness do not hinge on how others react toward us.

We then learn to love ourselves enough to detach ourselves from the way the world treats us. Whether it is with love or not, we can remain centered because of the trust and confidence we have in our self-love.

Detachment does not mean we are no longer interested in what other people think about us. It means that what they think does not affect our life one way or another. The reason we want to be in a powerful place such as this, is because life can change quickly, and searching outside of ourselves for worth and validation may leave us feeling empty if our worth or value is not found.

It is also important to detach from the way we want things to work out. If our self-worth is connected to a goal or milestone, and these are not accomplished, again our self-esteem tumbles. Here we return to our self-love for support. Imagine loving ourselves so much that no matter what happens in the physical world we still love ourselves. In this place of love, we accept that we did the best we could, and we know we did it with love in our heart.

Of course, we want all our attempts in life to succeed, but this isn't always the case. Some of our trials hold important lessons meant for our emotional growth. Even if we fail, we can find these lessons will benefit us in the future.

Detachment keeps us from judging ourselves harshly when things don't work out in our favor yet allows us to learn what we needed to learn, giving us the courage and strength to keep moving forward.

With these thoughts in mind, we may recognize that detachment is a form of separation, but it is also a way to connect with our self-love, found at the core of our being.

Depth

I REMEMBER WHEN I WAS LEARNING TO swim underwater. At first, I wanted to remain close to the surface. This felt the safest. But I soon realized there were things on the lakebed I wanted to see. This meant I would have to leave the comfort of the surface and dive into the unknown.

How deeply are we willing to look within ourselves to discover the truth of who we are? We may have to leave the comfort of our current reality, and go within, past our negative self-talk, the beliefs we were taught by others, and our self-doubt, to arrive at a place of true self-love.

Along this inner journey, we may come upon some uncomfortable memories. Yet, within each of these memories we will find the lessons we need to learn before we can live by our authentic truth.

The extent of our exploration will be determined by the depth of our desire to live to the fullness of who we are. This will take courage because we will have to look within ourselves to discover the self-love that will guide us along our emotional journey of self-realization.

It is the strength of our love for ourselves that will lead us along the path to knowing our true selves. Yet, if we know that love will be our guide, then the journey may not appear so challenging.

With each step along the road, love will be there to lead us.

This love then gives us the strength to look further and further into ourselves to discover who we are and what makes us truly happy and joyful. Think of it as loving ourselves so much we choose to free ourselves from a life filled with uncertainty and hesitation.

The depth of our self-discovery will be proportional to the strength of our courage and self-love. If for some reason we choose to remain at a certain level, we can still love ourselves for how far we have traveled.

Just as in learning to swim underwater, we can take it slowly, there is no need to rush. Getting comfortable with the process allows us a new sense of relief, giving us the ability to shed thoughts and beliefs that no longer serve us. Once here, we can look deeper within ourselves, searching for new clues to how we can live the best life possible.

The intention of this inner work is to understand the depth of love we have for ourselves. Even if we have never experienced this love, knowing self-love exists gives us something to work toward.

It is in the depth of our being where we realize the truth of who we are. As we sift through layers of self-doubt, negative self-talk, and false beliefs, we come face to face with our authentic self, and the love at the core of our being. From this awareness, we begin to live to the fullness of who we are.

This allows us to be true and honest with ourselves and others. We now know there is no reason to hide behind a false persona to protect ourselves. Our authentic self becomes the way we walk through life, the way we love, and the way we share ourselves with others.

In the depth of honesty and love, the world begins to change to match the love we share with those in our life. This is how we have a positive influence on the world. By having the courage to look within and realize that through our desire to heal from negative experiences, we can share the depth of our love without condition or expectation. We now have the courage to dive deep within ourselves, to recognize the freedom of our own true self-love, and the life this love gives us.

Discipline

When I think of the word discipline, I'm reminded of detention after school, or the quality time I spent with Mother Superior. As fun as it was getting into trouble, this type of discipline is not what this chapter is about.

Think of a time when an off-the-cuff comment spoken by a close friend sent you into an emotional tailspin. Although the words may have been hurtful, could you have found the discipline to remain emotionally centered? The discipline to stay balanced when life falls apart, or when someone speaks harmful words, is a form of self-control.

Yet discipline is also needed if we are going to begin the inner work of discovering the truth of who we are. It can be easy falling into the trap of believing we are just our physical body, and that's it. But as we begin the journey within, we will realize there is much more to our being than just our physicality.

Discipline allows us to silence the mental chatter and listen for the quiet voice of our true self-love, thereby giving us the inner stillness needed to hear the wisdom of our authentic self.

One of the challenges we face on our journey is dealing with the opinions of those who see our inner work as a waste of time. It is here where discipline is needed because we know that discovering our truth is important to our well-being, even if others do not.

I often think of philosopher Lao Tzu's quote, "The journey of a thousand miles begins with a single step." This is also true when it comes to our spiritual journey. These words remind us that we must place one foot in front of the other if we want to reach our destination. But at times we get tired or frustrated with our progress. To overcome this, we can look at how far we have traveled, and the discipline we counted on to help us along the way.

Each of us walks a different path through life, and we all face different distractions. The internet is a wonderful tool, yet it can also undermine our focus. This is where our discipline needs to be the strongest because we know time evaporates when we hit the search icon. Before we know it, we are far off topic, and have wasted much of our precious time.

The thought of being disciplined does not give us a warm, comfortable feeling. In a way, the importance of discipline makes us uncomfortable. One reason for this is when we are honest with ourselves, we can recognize how much time we have allowed to slip through our fingers, knowing we will never have that time back.

A thought to remember is discipline builds in strength over time. When we first begin our journey toward self-discovery, we may get frustrated with how little progress we appear to have made. We get impatient and might consider giving up all together. Not a very disciplined reaction, although understandable.

It is here we must think about our journey as changing old, outdated patterns of thought. We have been thinking these thoughts for many undisciplined years, so it will take time to unwind them from our consciousness. If our intention is to live to the fullness of who we are, we must recognize that many of our thoughts and behavioral patterns may have been created by experiences from which we have yet to heal.

If we choose to look within ourselves without self-judgement, and then decide to love ourselves, we will begin to develop the courage to be disciplined along our journey. In this place of discipline, we can silence our self-doubt, and ignore our negative self-talk, thereby allowing ourselves the ability to move forward without hesitation.

Even if our discipline falters from time to time, we will experience opportunities that teach us how to do better in the future. All we must do is know that by putting one foot in front of the other on the journey toward self-discovery, we will live to the fullness of who we are. Our discipline will carry us through, no matter what struggles or challenges we may face along the way.

Divine

Is it possible to recognize the Divine in the destitute? Those who do little for us, or those who do nothing for others? What prevents us from seeing the Divine everywhere we look, even in the mirror? Can we accept that when we reconnect with the truth of who we are, we will unite with the Divine?

Admitting the Divine is at the core of all we can see and beyond, allows us to move past our limiting beliefs. Yet the way we view the world is based on our thoughts and beliefs. If we believe it is only us humans on a lonely planet in the middle of nowhere, then we are blind to Divine presence.

In certain aspects of life, it may be easy to notice the Divine, when surrounded by nature, or with those we love. But when we are sitting on the bus, tired after long hours of work, or waiting in line at the grocery store, the Divine may appear absent.

Our search for the Divine must begin with a look in the mirror. The person staring back is the Divine in human form. Each of us is a reflection of the Divine. This may be a challenging thought because we believe our self-doubt and negative self-talk are the words of the Divine. Yet the Divine only expresses itself through love, kindness, and compassion.

When we contemplate the Divine existing in everyone, not only those with whom we agree, we struggle because we want the Divine to look, act, and speak, a certain way. We may have a preconceived idea of what the Divine should be. This image might not look or sound like anyone we know or see on the evening news. What if we were to acknowledge that at the core of our being, we are representations of the Divine? Even though we have lost our connection with this divinity?

Life can separate us from our authentic truth. We change who we are to please others, thereby living an existence not faithful to our purpose. This is not a genuine life. Our distractions as well as the expectations of others, have diverted us away from discovering our authentic truth, causing us to live a life absent of the knowing of our Divine self.

Although judgement has become common in today's society, it is another way we distance ourselves from the Divine. We judge to boost our self-esteem, making us feel better by criticizing others, giving us a false sense of superiority. To be one with our Divine nature, we must release our need for judgement by being more loving and kind.

As we become more accepting of others, we notice the Divine within ourselves, thereby allowing us to see Divine presence in the world around us. In doing so, we align with the love that is the essence of who we are. It is this love that unites each of us with the Divine.

We may be afraid to think of a source of Divine energy. This thought asks us to contemplate something bigger than ourselves, something larger than we can imagine. Yet when we realize the magnitude of the Divine, there is no reason to fear. In this state of acceptance, we realize our bond with each other and the natural world.

To live to the fullness of who we are, is to recognize the Divine guidance offered to us at every turn. It may seem odd to think of our intuition as originating from the Divine, yet through this union, we understand that our intuitive feelings are messages from this powerful source of love.

The intention of our journey through life is to reconnect with the love at the core of our being. This connection unites us with the Divine. It is in this state of awareness we begin to live an authentic life.

E

Easy

Oh, HOW WE WISH WE COULD just snap our fingers to make life easy. Although, if it were easy would it be worthwhile? Have we chosen the easy way out only to discover more difficulties later in life? In situations like these, we may realize that easy is not always easy.

Our life is full of lessons if we are aware enough to notice. Deep within the struggles we often face are the keys we need to move toward our best life possible. Although if we choose the easy path, we may never learn how to unlock our full potential.

Life is interesting because at times we ignore our responsibility toward ourselves and blame others for the way life is unfolding. This serves no useful purpose except to avoid doing the inner work of seeking the truth of who we are.

Yet if we think blaming others is easy, we must understand that the negativity of blame begins to control us. The reason why we blame others for the way life is turning out, is because we fail to notice the life lesson their behavior is teaching us.

It takes true courage to take a step back with the intention of learning from those who challenge us, and the experiences they have put us through. But if we accept that the meaning of life is to live to the fullness of who we are, then we must forgo the easy road, for the more difficult road of self-examination.

At first, we may not want to look too deeply within ourselves because we believe we will discover aspects of ourselves we find uncomfortable. Yet we have much to learn from these unexplored areas of who we are. Is this inner work easy? Probably not, although nothing of lasting value comes from making easy choices.

When we begin the journey within, we notice that one of the challenges we often face is accepting responsibility for our actions, as well as our reactions to those who trigger us emotionally. Being responsible for our inner peace may not be easy, but this is the only true way to live an authentic life.

This might be counterintuitive, but the more responsibility we take for our own life, the easier life becomes. At first speaking up for our needs may seem intimidating. Yet if we take the easy route and remain silent, others will assume our needs, and their assumption may not suit our best interest. Although remaining silent may appear easy, accepting responsibility for our well-being is a true act of self-love.

A difficult aspect of life is to learn what is true and right for us. This involves much trial and error, although there is always an opportunity to learn something beneficial from every experience. It may not be easy, but with careful attention to what brings us true, authentic happiness, we will gain the knowledge and wisdom needed to live to the fullness of who we are.

Once we realize what brings us true joy, we will have the strength to steer our life in a meaningful direction, thereby giving ourselves the best chance to align with the fullness of who we are.

Choosing this path may not be easy, although in doing so we will live a life closer to our authentic truth than had we chosen the easier course of action.

Embodiment

At times the spiritual journey can be challenging. We are faced with many ideas that may not align with the truth we are experiencing. Yet if we are to connect with our authenticity, we must become the embodiment of the positive lessons we are learning along the path to knowing our true self.

The intention of a spiritual journey, or the work of becoming our authentic self, is to match our thoughts and beliefs with our words and actions. There can be no difference between thought and action if we want to embody the truth of our higher self.

When we look at true masters, no matter what their craft or skill, their mastery is interwoven into every aspect of their daily lives. There is no separation between their mastery and who they present to the world. They embody the truth of who they are in thought, word, and action.

As we start down the road to embodying self-mastery, we must clear away the thoughts and beliefs that no longer serve a useful purpose. These thoughts and beliefs are often deeply engrained in who we show to the world. They have become such a part of who we think we are, it can be difficult to unwind them from our identity.

Isn't that the point of discovering the truth of who we are? To find the core of our being, thereby living by this truth?

When we think, speak, and act in alignment with our truth, we will embody the love that is the foundation of all life.

Think of the positive effect we will have on the world when we are the embodiment of truth and love. Our every thought, word, and action will be in alignment with this powerful source of love.

When we embody the eternal love found within us, there will be no need to hide behind the façade our ego often creates. We no longer judge others to make ourselves feel better, because we accept that everyone is doing the best they can. If and when we do judge, we quickly realize that we must look within ourselves to ask why we have chosen this negative behavior to express ourselves.

To embody this powerful love is to master the way we interact with the world. Our thoughts will originate from a place of love, thereby allowing love to be the foundation of all our words and actions. This is the embodiment of a true spiritual journey, to discover the love within us, and then to live by this love.

If we consider love as a higher level of consciousness, then when we embody love, we are in an elevated state of consciousness. This allows us to access the wisdom of this higher realm of awareness. It is here where we can tap into the guidance shared by our higher self, thereby living a life of truth, wisdom, and honesty.

Many of the challenges we face along the journey of self-discovery may be of our own making. Self-doubt, negative self-talk, and fear can play a key role in our lack of success. But if we know ahead of time, as we do now, that the final destination is to embody love, we can keep moving forward no matter what our fear, or mental chatter tells us.

As we live a life of love, we align with our authenticity. We then love ourselves enough to speak our truth to the world without fear, or hesitation. This is the embodiment of who we are, and the love we have come to know as true.

Encouragement

It takes nothing away from us when we encourage others to live to the fullness of who they are. Our words could be the fuel needed to help them move past the roadblocks keeping them from pursuing their dreams. Yet, we often keep from expressing our support for one reason or another.

Do we realize our words of encouragement can make the difference between a life well lived, or one that falls short? Think of a time when the encouraging words of a close friend made all the difference. They could have remained silent, but instead chose to speak in a manner that benefited our journey.

In truth, speaking words of encouragement is an act of self-confidence and love. Self-confidence, because we know that no matter how successful a person is, their success takes nothing away from anyone. Nor are we threatened by their success. Love, because we love ourselves enough to convey our words of encouragement without the expectation of a reward for our kindness.

For some of us, sharing encouraging words might not come easily. One reason could be because of the life we have experienced. We may have failed too often and do not want to see others go through the pain of failure; therefore we remain silent.

To live an authentic life is to understand that life is all about the lessons we choose to learn. There will be lessons in our successes as well as in our failures. Either way there will be growth from these experiences.

At times we may not be enthusiastic about the choices others make. This should not stop us from encouraging them to keep moving forward. No one can see another person's dream as clearly as they do. With this in mind, we do them a disservice if we try to persuade them to go in a different direction.

It is not only those around us who need encouragement, we need it as well. If our dream aligns with our authentic self, we owe it to ourselves to pursue it as far as we can. It may end in failure or success; we have no idea. Yet we cannot allow our fears to stop us if our dreams feel true and right. It is much healthier to walk into the unknown, than it is to regret not taking the steps necessary to accomplish our goals.

We often think we need constant encouragement to carry us through the entire process. It might be beneficial to break our dreams down into little pieces, this way we empower ourselves because of our small successes. Each step forward should encourage us to take another step. Even if we cannot see the entire path clearly, we can encourage ourselves to make the next move.

There will be occasions when we lose motivation or feel demoralized. It is here we can look back and recognize how far we have come. It seems the toughest part of climbing a mountain is when we get close to the top. Our fatigue may cause us to contemplate turning around. Yet when we see how far we have traveled, we may decide to keep moving forward, the summit might be closer than we think.

There will be occasions when life will not be easy. If we take it one moment at a time, we will muster the inner strength to remain focused on our dreams and goals. In situations such as these, we must be our own cheering section, encouraging ourselves even when life gets tough. We must also encourage ourselves when life gets easy, it is in times like these when we lose focus and end up making costly mistakes.

To live an authentic life may be difficult in a world that asks us to fit in. If we want to realize our true potential, while seeing others doing the same, it is our responsibility to encourage ourselves and those around us to look past the beliefs that limit our successes. Thereby giving us the best opportunity to live a fulfilling life.

Expectations

EXPECTATIONS CAN COVER A WIDE RANGE of emotions. We often have an expectation that things will work out in our favor. When they do, our emotions are high, filling us with positive energy.

We also expect people to behave in a way that pleases us. When their actions don't meet our expectations, we feel let down, disappointed in them, flooding us with negative energy. Our expectations are crushed, and their behavior ends up hurting us.

When we look closer at expectations, we notice they originate from a desire to control the outcome of a situation. We want things to work out a certain way. When they do, we are pleased. If not, we are hurt.

This can be challenging when it comes to maintaining our inner peace, because through our expectations, we attach our state of calm to the actions of others. In a way our expectations allow things we cannot control to rule over us emotionally.

If we were to separate ourselves from the expectation that others will behave in a way that pleases us, we distance ourselves from having our emotions controlled by their actions. The best we can do is to learn how to control our reaction toward the behavior of others.

We have expectations of things always working out for us. Yet the outcome may be very different than what we had expected. At times our expectations can limit the possibilities that exist. We want things to fit into our expectations yet while doing so, we block the possibility of something better coming our way. Whatever the outcome, for our emotional growth, we must look for the positive lessons within these experiences.

One of the lessons we often overlook, at the core of our being, is a source of unconditional love that knows no boundaries, has no limitations, and does not place expectations on others. It is because of this love we understand that everyone is doing the best they can.

When we place an expectation on someone, we may be asking them to behave in a way that may not be possible. By accepting that everyone is doing the best they can at any moment in their day, we release our need to make them responsible for fulfilling our expectations. In doing so we accept them for who they are, without the unnecessary burden of our expectations.

To take it a step further, think of loving ourselves enough so the actions of others no longer bother our inner peace. Through this understanding, we recognize that their behavior reflects who they are and the inner struggles they may be fighting. While our reaction to them, or any challenging situation, is a reflection of who we are, the depth of our self-love, and the inner struggles we may be facing as well.

By freeing ourselves from the need to place expectations on ourselves and others, we begin to enjoy more inner peace, and healthier relationships. Our emotional state of being will no longer be attached to an expectation of how we want things to work out. We now know there is always something better for us when we release our need for expectations while allowing unlimited possibilities to flow into our life.

F

Failure

W<small>HY</small> <small>WOULD</small> <small>ANYONE</small> <small>WRITING</small> <small>A</small> <small>BOOK</small> such as this include a chapter on failure? The reason is because failure can be one of the best teachers we may ever have. If we are aware, we will recognize the important lessons in each of our failures. These are the lessons that will be the most beneficial to our emotional and spiritual growth.

How many of us have a fear of failure? We don't want to look incompetent in front of others or add to any insecurities we may already have. For this reason, we may not try anything new or something that may challenge us. Yet how does this make us feel about ourselves? If we don't try, aren't we letting ourselves down?

Successful people will speak of the hours they spend improving themselves. Athletes devote extra time on the court. Musicians talk of the hours practicing the most challenging parts of a certain piece of music, while writers, write pages and pages with no intention of having them published. All with the purpose of not failing in public.

Yet if we knew the work successful people put in, we would see that in their practice time, they were indeed failing. At the same time, they are learning from their failures. As frightening as this sounds, to be successful we *have* to fail.

If we are afraid of failure, we may never take the steps to succeed. But what kind of life does that leave us? A life of uncomfortable comfort? Uncomfortable because at some emotional level we realize our fear controls us. This fear has prevented us from living to the fullness of who we are.

To be comfortable with our fear is a subtle sign of our fear of failure as well. The thing about comfort is that it is a choice. We choose to be comfortable with our fear of failure. Thereby allowing our fear to dictate the outcome of our life.

Think for a moment, how life would be if those who did great things that benefited humanity allowed their fear of failure to stop them? Would we have cured diseases? Built bridges across mighty rivers? What about flying from continent to continent while reading a book, drinking a glass of wine? Just about everything you can think of was created, or invented by someone who looked their fear of failure in the eye and kept moving forward anyway.

Did these people fail? Of course, but they learned something in the process, and then used this knowledge to improve themselves, and the systems they were creating. Once again, we realize that to be successful, failure is part of the process. We don't have to get comfortable with failure, but we should see failure as an opportunity to gain much needed wisdom that will help us in the future.

Two things successful people have is courage and stamina. Courage to work through their self-doubt and negative self-talk. And stamina to keep moving forward when things seem impossible.

All of us have courage and stamina. We just need to believe in ourselves enough that we can count on them when we need their support. It does take courage and stamina to pick ourselves up after failure and continue to move toward our goals.

But if our intention is to live our best life then we can be grateful for the presence of our courage and stamina.

Is failure painful? Yes! Will failure challenge us emotionally? Again yes! Would it be possible to benefit from the failure that causes our growth? Most definitely! Will failure be scary? Not as scary as sitting on the couch asking ourselves how life would have turned out if we had just silenced our self-doubt and were willing to accept failure as part of the process.

Fear

Why do we consider fear an emotion that will prevent us from living to the fullness of who we are? What if we were to look at our fears as messengers with important lessons for our emotional growth? In seeing fear this way, we disarm its ability to keep us in our comfort zone.

Is it possible to overcome our fear with knowledge and wisdom? The more we know, the less ability our fear has to control us. By challenging our fear this way, we then have the inner strength to silence our fear, allowing us to learn what we need to move forward toward the life of our dreams.

If we are afraid of starting something new, or traveling down an unknown path, our fear will stop us. But wouldn't it be best to learn as much as we could about our choices? Thereby minimizing the impact fear has on the outcome of our decisions.

By observing our reaction to fear, we notice we often withdraw emotionally, doing what we can to protect ourselves from the unknown. If we behave this way, we limit what we can learn from the experience. To learn from our fear, we must remain receptive to the information our fear holds. If we want to react to the best of our ability, uncovering the root cause of our fear will be beneficial to the outcome.

When we are well informed, we are rarely afraid. I learned to rock climb at a young age. I took lessons to learn the latest safety techniques. Even though the sport looks dangerous to the untrained eye, with proper education, climbing rock can be relatively safe. I had no fear of climbing high off the ground, because I trusted the rope, and used my knowledge to make my climb as safe as possible.

At times our fear may be justified. It can be easy to succumb to the negative energy of fear, limiting our ability to remain emotionally centered. If we allow fear to control us, we are paralyzed, ready to give up without learning anything that will help move us forward.

Can we look past our fear, to see what it is we must learn from this powerful emotion? The way forward is through learning as much as we can about the causes of our fear. In treating fear this way we are not held hostage by an emotion we can minimize through expanding our knowledge and wisdom.

As with any emotion there are two sides to fear. One side stops us in our tracks, because we are afraid of failing. We are fearful of stepping away from our comfort zone so why start anyway? The other, more productive side of fear, is we are afraid of failing so we learn as much as we can, then use this information to succeed.

Another aspect of fear we may contend with is the fear other people will express to us. They may fear our journey because they have remained in place throughout their life. They fear the unknown, thereby projecting this fear onto us. If we are feeling insecure, we accept their fear, hindering our ability to live truthfully.

Even though we may love those around us, we must learn to ignore their fears. Oftentimes they argue in support of their fears, offering no alternative solutions. This doesn't mean we have to accept their limiting beliefs.

Certain fears can be valid. Yet, when fear is shared by others it comes from their level of awareness. Those who have never rock climbed only see the danger, they do not understand the safety procedures. They project their fear onto us, assuming they are looking out for our best interest. Their fear may have little truth when it comes to the choices we have made.

Our ability to break our fears into small pieces gives us the opportunity to see the exact causes of our fears. This will give us the focus to concentrate on what really worries us. Then we can work through these concerns, allowing us to move through our fears quickly.

Fear can be a stubborn teacher, helping us reach a quality of life we once thought unimaginable. Fear can also prevent us from being authentic. Living to the fullness of who we are will hinge on having the courage to uncover the lessons found within our fears.

Forgiveness

IT IS SAID THAT FORGIVENESS IS a powerful tool for our emotional healing. Yet, why is it so hard to forgive? Do we want those who harmed us to suffer the same pain they placed on us? Does holding a grudge actually make us feel better? We often forget that through forgiveness we free ourselves from those who have caused our pain.

If we look closer at the idea of forgiveness, we realize we forgive because we are tired of carrying the weight of the painful memory. We want to move on, but as long as we keep the memory active in our consciousness we are anchored in place. Once we realize we are stuck emotionally, we may recognize that to forgive is to set ourselves free.

The root of forgiveness is love, a love we have for ourselves. We choose to forgive because we love ourselves enough to free ourselves from the burden of our emotional pain. This allows us to return to the life we once knew, a life founded on love.

If it is too challenging to forgive those who caused the pain, is it possible to forgive ourselves for carrying the emotional burden of the experience? Some would say there is no reason to forgive ourselves, but there is often guilt and shame, interwoven in the pain we have experienced. By forgiving ourselves we release these negative feelings from our awareness. Others may have caused our suffering, but we may have placed the guilt and shame on ourselves.

The act of self-forgiveness also helps us accept that we were doing the best we could at the time. This acceptance removes any harsh self-judgement we may hold. Given what we knew at the time we did the best we could. If we had known more, things may have turned out differently, although we now realize that self-forgiveness is the path to our emotional freedom, and healing.

When people think of forgiveness, they think they must have the bully over for dinner or speak face to face with the one who caused the injustice. This is not the case. Such a meeting may only add more pain to the situation. People also believe an apology will begin the healing process, but if an apology is not given, then healing will be on hold until one is received.

Through the act of forgiveness there is no need to interact with those who harmed us. We can forgive within ourselves and move on from there. If we see them at a later time, they will know we have separated ourselves from them emotionally. Our forgiveness will give us the strength to stand tall within our self-love.

The more we encourage the growth of our self-love, the more aware we will be of the negative impact of seeking revenge. We realize this negative behavior will only deepen our connection to the pain we have suffered, and those who caused this pain.

To forgive requires courage, stamina, and love, because it may be easy to fall back into old patterns of thought. Although these patterns may be comfortable, they serve us no useful purpose if our desire is to move toward a healthier, self-loving life.

By choosing to forgive, we turn away from the negativity of anger and resentment, toward a state of consciousness that is more loving and kind. We can do little about the past, although through the act of forgiveness we enter into an awareness of our self-love found in the present moment.

The intention of forgiveness is to set ourselves free, free from the burden of a situation that may have been out of our control, and free to love ourselves for having the courage to forgive.

Freedom

How free are we? I'm not talking about having to pay taxes, or our other responsibilities. I'm talking about the freedom to choose our attitude no matter what happens in life. If we make the right choices this freedom will cost us nothing. If we choose the wrong attitude, it may cost us more than we are willing to accept.

Freedom is an interesting thing. We often think we are free, yet when we look closely, we will notice we are attached to the beliefs we carry within our consciousness. Do these beliefs give us freedom, or do they keep us from realizing the fullness of who we are?

Our beliefs create the way we experience life. If they are based on love, kindness, and compassion, we will walk through life free to enjoy these powerful emotions. Yet if our beliefs are focused on the negatives, we choose to see around us, then we are trapped by this negative energy.

A good way to tell whether or not we are free is to observe our reaction to the challenges we often face in our day. Do these challenges control us emotionally? If my dog barks in the night, causing me to get upset, then my negative reaction to my dog being a dog, controls me. In this case I am not free, I am a prisoner of my negative emotions.

If I accept that my dog is doing his job, his barking a warning, then my reaction to his barking will be different. I may become grateful for his signal that something is amiss. This way I am free from any negativity.

Think of freedom this way, the more loving and kind we are, the more freedom we will experience. Yet, when we are angry, resentful, or bitter, we are controlled by our negativity. This way of thinking gives us the opportunity to recognize that love is the ultimate source of freedom. The deeper our love, the freer we are to live an authentic life.

One reason we may not feel free is we often attach our peace of mind to the behavior of others. If their actions please us, we are happy. When they don't please us, we become angry or disappointed. Happiness based on how others behave will lead us on an emotional rollercoaster ride.

The depth of our freedom will come down to the choices we make. We can choose to allow others to live as they please, or we can try to control their behavior, which will never make us happy, or bring us any lasting peace. The freedom to choose our attitude toward others is a powerful choice. But we often forget it is a choice.

No matter the situation we have the freedom to choose how we will react. Do we understand that the outcome of any situation will be determined by the attitude we freely choose? We could justify our negative behavior by saying it is in reaction to the circumstances surrounding a situation. This may be true, but does this negative behavior benefit us in any way?

When we realize we are free to choose our attitude, we accept responsibility for the way we approach life. Yet we often try to avoid this responsibility by blaming others for our negative attitude, and how unhappy we feel. We are then held captive by our need to blame others for the negativity in our life.

To be truly free is to accept that how life unfolds will be

based on the love in our heart, how we share this love, and the attitude we choose when things don't work out as we had planned.

G

Gifts

Have you ever stopped to think of the gifts you give to the world? Whether it is a kind word, letting someone merge ahead of you into traffic, or helping someone load their groceries into their car; gifts come in many forms. Not all gifts are purchased on the internet.

When we think of gifts, giving and receiving gifts during special occasions comes to mind. Yet how often do we consider our everyday acts of kindness as gifts? Some of these acts might seem small to us but may have a big impact on the lives of others.

A true gift should be given freely, without conditions attached. If we give a gift with an expectation of a reward, or a change in behavior, the gift has not been given from the heart. We may try to please our unruly children with a gift if they promise to behave. This type of gift, loaded with conditions and expectations, could be regarded as a bribe.

Oftentimes the best gifts are those given without much thought. These spontaneous acts of kindness have a foundation rooted in love. When we give these gifts freely, we do so with no strings attached. They are honest expressions of our authentic self.

Gifts founded in love come in different shapes and sizes. We can sit with a friend who is in pain without saying a word, our presence a gift. Or we can help an elderly neighbor around their house. It is in these situations where our inner flow of love radiates from us, easing any uncertainty or insecurities others might be experiencing.

We may think our gifts are rooted in love, but we must look at our motivation behind the gift. Are we giving from the heart, or are we sacrificing ourselves to boost our ego, or to elevate our self-worth? Afterwards saying to ourselves, "Look what I gave them, they should be grateful for my sacrifice." Notice the difference between this behavior and giving a loving gift without attachment.

What if we were to consider our presence here on Earth a gift to the world? Not a self-serving kind of gift, just the gift of our authentic self, freely expressed. As we begin the journey of discovering the truth of who we are, we also notice how unique we are. This uniqueness is our gift to those around us.

We can give many material gifts, purchased with a few clicks on the computer. But the gift that will have a lasting effect will be the gift of unconditional love. Material things will wear out or may be misplaced, but the warmth of unconditional love will last a lifetime.

By living an authentic life, we are giving the gift of our true self to the world. This is a gift founded on love. A gift such as this will have a positive impact on the lives of everyone we meet. As time goes by people may forget our name, but they will always remember the gift of unconditional love we shared with them as we walked together through life.

Grace

THERE ARE TIMES WHEN THE WORLD can be harsh and unkind. Yet do we have to retaliate? Is it possible to maintain a state of grace as we go through life?

Imagine the love of all creation filling our being, radiating from us as we walk down the street. We share our love freely with no need to judge or ridicule others. This is the foundation of grace.

Each of us is living a life that may not make sense to other people. It can be easy to notice our differences that overshadow our commonalities. We have something in common with all people including those who appear less fortunate than us. When we accept this, we are in a state of grace.

The hard thing about maintaining our state of grace is we often want others to behave in a way that pleases us. In having this mindset, our emotional state of being will always be controlled by the actions of others.

Yet to be in a position to experience grace we must understand that everyone is doing the best they can. Our grace recognizes their challenges, allowing us to be compassionate and empathetic. Although it can be easy to judge, we do not ask anyone to measure up to the unrealistic standards of society.

Grace has a foundation built on love. We may not think we are loving when we have no need to judge, but we are. Love teaches us that any negative thought, word, or action separates us from our inner grace.

When we move away from our addiction to negativity, we elevate our consciousness. In this place of awareness, we begin to live a life filled with grace. This may not be easy to sustain, because we can easily fall back into old patterns of thought and behavior.

Once we become aware of how living a life of grace feels, we will notice if we have strayed away from our inner love. When we realize that to live to the fullness of who we are is to live a grace-filled life, we become conscious of how we treat ourselves and those around us.

As we go through life in a graceful state of being, we will notice how connected we are to an eternal source of unconditional love. Living a life of grace is being guided by this powerful love.

Grace is a butterfly gently touching our skin, causing us to see the beauty within all beings, continuing on to touch others, sparking awe and joy within them. We marvel at the butterfly's strength, and ability to fly gracefully in a world filled with obstacles and unforeseen challenges.

It makes no difference if you are a man or a woman, true grace has no limitations, no boundaries. Grace is gentle, yet strong, compassionate and forgiving, loving and kind, in the most challenging of situations.

At the core of our being is love. Sharing this love without conditions or expectations, is the true nature of grace. There is no value in hoarding our love, this will limit the way we experience love for ourselves and those in our life. Living a life of grace, we will realize there is no lack of love. Our love is unlimited in every way. It is our perception of a lack of love that will distance us from our eternal source of grace.

Our state of grace is a gift we give to ourselves and the world. As our grace touches others, we connect with the love at the core of their being, even if they are unaware of this love. Grace transcends all physical and emotional barriers.

While walking through life, our grace is a prayer of thanks for the abundance we see in the world. Living a life founded on grace is living a life of gratitude. It is in this state of grace we unite with the truth of who we are.

Gratitude

MOST OF THE TIME WE EXPRESS gratitude for the things that have worked out in our favor. This is easy. If we want to live to the fullness of who we are, we must also express gratitude for the things that didn't work out.

If we were to look over our past, we may see jobs, relationships, and opportunities that weren't right for us. If we stayed in these situations how would life have turned out? Can we be grateful for the lessons these experiences taught us?

Years ago, I had a business that fell apart. At the time I was frustrated as well as disappointed. Not long after I left the partnership, I began to realize how fortunate I was that things ended as they did. I became grateful for what I learned and the connections I made.

To arrive at a place of gratitude for our failures or mistakes, we must first release our anger and our need to blame others for how things unfolded. I had to accept my responsibility for my role in the situation. I knew if I wanted to succeed in the future, blame was not an option.

It can take time to arrive at an emotional state of gratitude when things don't turn out like we had planned. However, if we take a closer look, we will find many beneficial lessons within these experiences. These lessons will give us the wisdom and strength to continue on in the future.

One thing about gratitude, the more we focus our attention on what makes us grateful, we will find more things worthy of our gratitude. It's a funny thing because at times we believe there is nothing in life to be grateful about. But if we take an honest look, we will begin to see more positive reasons to be grateful.

Building a mindset founded on gratitude is a lot like climbing a ladder. With each step we get higher and higher. With each expression of gratitude, we elevate our emotional state of mind, thereby allowing us to recognize more reasons why we should be grateful. This will give us an emotional boost of energy.

I can think of a number of situations that didn't end in my favor, but I'm grateful for having gone through these experiences. It is the lessons I learned from these situations where I could find reasons to be grateful. Even if I was grateful for the smallest thing, I could build upon this one thing, then move up emotionally from there.

Expressing gratitude for the cool stuff in life is easy. It's when we learn to be grateful for the struggles we often face, that we begin to enjoy the benefits of a life filled with gratitude. The challenges that come our way help create who we see in the mirror each day. By learning to be grateful for these difficulties, we will discover the truth of who we are.

Guidance

Why is it we often look to others for guidance? Is it because we don't trust ourselves? Don't we know the advice we receive from them will be based on *their* life experiences, and may not be true and right for us? If we want guidance that is best for us, we must look within ourselves.

The challenge becomes one of knowing where to find the guidance. Our mind is full of thoughts and beliefs that may not serve our best interests. Our head can also be filled with the chatter of our self-doubt and negative self-talk. This is why it can be confusing when it comes to choosing what is best for us. Our thoughts get in the way.

The guidance that will be the most accurate for any choice we make will be a feeling found within us. This guidance is our intuition, instincts, and gut feelings. These intuitive feelings are often overlooked when it comes to making the life choices we are faced with each day.

The thing about our intuition is it may be overpowered by the guidance we believe is true, spoken by our ego. Yet the ego does not always have our best interest as its main focus. Many times the ego guides us in a direction that only satisfies the ego. We may think the ego leads us on the right path, but are we happy when we arrive at our destination?

One way to know if we are following true guidance or our

ego, is to ask which guidance is founded on love. Not a love of money, power, or prestige, but a love for ourselves.

Our intuitive guidance knows us better than we know ourselves. This guidance is always looking out for our health and well-being. In comparison, the ego guides us toward what will make the ego pleased with itself.

I remember a time when I ignored my intuitive guidance, and followed the path my ego chose. I knew I should have followed my intuition, but I didn't want to shame myself in front of my friends. As it turned out, my gut feeling was right, and I should have followed its loving guidance.

Yet, this is how we learn if the guidance we receive is right for us. By acknowledging the intuitive feelings, and deciding if we should follow them or not, the final outcome will reveal if we made the right choice. In my case, following my intuition would have saved me from a few nights in the hospital.

When it comes to trusting the wisdom of those close to us, we must always remember that only *we* know what is true and right for us. Our friends and family may love us and have an opinion as to which direction we should choose, but we alone will walk this path. In the end, the outcome of our life is our responsibility.

A simple way to learn to trust our inner guidance is to ask ourselves which choice is right for us. Begin with a simple yes or no question: "Should I fly or drive?" Then ask again, switching it to no or yes. When we hear or feel an answer, move in that direction. We are looking for an answer that resonates deeply within us. An answer filled with a loving understanding of our health and well-being.

Experience will be the teacher if we made the right choice. As confidence builds, we can move on to more challenging decisions. True guidance coming from within will always have a foundation of love, and a concern for our best interest as its priority. Following our inner guidance will be the best thing we can do for a life filled with true and lasting joy.

Haters

No MATTER WHAT WE TRY TO accomplish in life, there will always be those who criticize us. They may say we had it easier than they did. They may complain about the breaks we had, while bragging about the challenges that broke them.

Haters hate us because they believe our upbringing was better than theirs, even though we may have been raised in the same household. On and on it goes, it can be endless. It seems people who behave this way hold a grudge against us for some unknown reason. These people are our haters.

As much as I don't like the word, the description fits. If we look closely, we will notice they hate us because we are not allowing our life challenges to hinder our progress or define who we are.

Maybe we took a workshop to improve our skills which made us more valuable to an employer, and this irritated them. Did we start the business they always imagined, but were too afraid to step into the unknown? Is it possible they hate us because we have accepted responsibility for our healing causing our life to change for the better?

Haters are always attempting to bring us down, while trying to raise themselves up. They often feel we have it easier than they do, yet they fail to do the work needed to elevate their worth.

Speaking hateful words toward another person is easy.

These words are often filled with anger, resentment, and jealousy. They require little thought. When we listen to the words haters speak, we realize these words reflect what is going on within them emotionally.

There is a saying that goes, "You will always be criticized by those who are doing less than you." This means our haters are not on the same playing field as we are. Yet, they don't see it this way. All they see is our success, thereby hating us for it.

To be successful at anything takes hard work and dedication. Oftentimes success doesn't come easy. There will be setbacks, failures, and those who secretly hope we fall on our face. Whatever the outcome, we must deal with the challenges life hands us, as well as those who hate us.

Haters come in all shapes and sizes. They can be coworkers, people at the gym, people we don't know, and sadly, family members. They can even be those who read our books, shop at our stores, or support our businesses. People will hate us just because we are successful.

Many haters believe when a person is successful, they take something away from others. This mindset is a consciousness of lack. The world in which we live has unlimited possibilities. When we are on the path to living an authentic life, we can take advantage of opportunities anyone can access. Yet some people are too afraid to do so.

It takes courage to walk into the unknown while pursuing a dream. We must recognize the possibilities, then take the necessary steps to see them come to fruition. Success doesn't just happen. It is important to take action to be successful.

Haters would rather pull us down to their level because they lack the confidence to move away from their comfort zone. They are too afraid to attempt to live beyond their wild-est dreams, although they wish they had the courage to do so.

When we take a closer look at the hater mindset, we notice they lack awareness of their own self-love. They act as they do because it makes them feel better about themselves. Haters get an emotional rush from their behavior; this justifies their actions.

Realizing haters are disconnected from their own self-love means they are also separated from their authentic self. Yet they hate us because we are living a life of grace and authenticity, one of true meaning and purpose.

If we hate our haters, we are no better than our haters. One way to overcome the energy of our haters is through the love at the core of our being. Just because they hate us, doesn't mean we should hate them. The best we can do for anyone is to love them without conditions or expectations.

Sure, it can be difficult to love our haters. But in doing so we remain true to ourselves. This gives us the strength to accept that haters are doing the best they can. It also teaches us that our judgement of them diminishes our ability to love ourselves.

Rather than become involved in an emotional battle with haters, accept the lessons they are teaching. This prevents us from falling into the trap of being separated from the truth of our authentic self.

Honesty

Are we living an honest life? I'm not asking if we're criminals. I'm asking if we're living by the truth of who we are. We spend much time telling ourselves the life we are living is aligned with our truth, but is this so? To live an honest life is to work through our false beliefs with the intention of uncovering the authentic truth found at the core of our being. Then to live by this realization.

It can be easy to trick ourselves into thinking an unsatisfying life is right for us. One reason may be because doing the inner work to discover our authentic self seems too difficult. With each new realization, our self-doubt may raise its ugly head, preventing us from moving further along our journey. Yet when we take an honest look at our self-doubt, we will notice much of our doubt is a lie we tell ourselves because we are not strong enough to challenge our insecurities.

Our negative self-talk is not a true representation of who we are either. It may be just a louder, more convincing voice of self-doubt. Neither our negative self-talk nor our self-doubt will give us an honest assessment of our true potential. Only our self-love is capable of that.

To live to the fullness of who we are, we must first learn to love ourselves unconditionally. This means to love ourselves no matter what our self-judgement is telling us, whatever the outcome of any situation.

When we are honest with ourselves, we understand that everything happening to us is an opportunity for our emotional growth. Yet it takes courage to see life this way, because it can be easy to surrender the responsibility for our own happiness to those who have caused our discomfort.

Being honest with ourselves is knowing we will never live a truly authentic life if we ask others to be responsible for our physical and emotional well-being. This may be a challenge to accept because we are surrounded by people we trust, and their behavior does affect us emotionally. However, we have a choice to allow their actions to upset us or not. To be honest with ourselves is to know we have a choice in how we react to the way others treat us.

It is here we return to our self-love, because when we are honest and love ourselves, we realize we will always be emotionally supported by our self-love. This gives us the strength and wisdom to remain centered when things fall apart. It also allows us to understand that everyone is doing the best they can at any given moment in their life. When we accept this powerful truth, we will release our need to judge others, or criticize their behavior.

As we begin the journey of being honest with ourselves, we will know what is true and right for us by how the thought of it makes us feel. This is where we learn to trust our intuition to guide us to the best possible life. We often try to fool ourselves into thinking we can't trust our intuition. In doing so, we are denying ourselves an honest source of guidance that will never lead us astray.

Living an honest life is a life based on our true self-love and the courage to live to the fullness of who we are. It is in this powerful emotional state of being where our honesty will help us overcome any obstacle we may face along the journey of life.

Humility

THERE IS A COMMON MISCONCEPTION THAT to be humble we must be a doormat, on which to allow others to wipe their muddy feet. When we examine this idea of humility, we notice there is a complete lack of self-love. We cannot claim to love ourselves while we let others treat us poorly. This behavior is neither authentic, nor are we being humble.

We often think the way to gain acceptance is to brag or boast about our accomplishments. The focus becomes more about boosting our image through what we have achieved than being in alignment with our authentic self. Real, honest humility does not need to show off because the truth of who we are speaks without words.

Sure, we all want to tell the world about the wonderful things we have done in life. But if we use this as an opportunity to measure ourselves against others, we are not being authentic, nor are we being humble. In a way, we brag to publicize our own self-worth.

Honest humility allows us to use what we have learned from our successes and failures to build our confidence. Thereby giving us the ability to empower those who are struggling to find their own successes when life challenges them.

We may not realize it, but when we boast or brag, we cause others to remain silent or feel insecure. Our words have the power to harm or heal. Those in need of support will often turn away from our advice because our behavior does not align with our authenticity.

This is when we must look within ourselves to ask why we are behaving as we are. Is there a root cause for our need to boast? Oftentimes the reason is a lack of true self-love, a love found deep within us. At times we think our bragging is a sign of self-love, but this is not self-loving humility.

True humility gives us the strength to see the importance of our accomplishments, yet we also recognize the need to be kind to others. No one feels good after being the center of another's bragging rant. After such an episode we often feel drained and doubt our value.

Humility is a state of awareness based on self-love. We love ourselves enough to know that constantly being the center of attention will never bring us any inner peace. If we have a need for outside validation, we are not aligned with our authentic self.

Imagine loving ourselves so deeply that anything can happen in the outside world, giving us the courage to remain true to ourselves. We choose to stay centered rather than fall into the abyss of negativity, or changing who we are to receive praise from others. Humility is a strength not a weakness, offering us the insight to know who we are, why we are placed in certain situations, and how to act when these situations fall apart.

The world is full of people who will tell us what they have accomplished, yet how do they act when we don't care what they have done? Many people live for the spotlight, sharing their escapades on social media in search of likes and followers. Yet how many of these people would continue to behave as they do if social media were to disappear this very instant?

To be humble is to live a life guided by the love found

deep within us, then doing what is needed to change the world through this love each and every day.

Humble people do not expect thanks after helping those who are less fortunate. They do so because it aligns with the truth of who they are. They behave this way because they love themselves enough to do the right thing, even if no one is watching or listening.

Humility teaches us that at any moment the tide could turn, causing life to be completely different. It is in these situations authentic people learn to respect those who have faced unseen challenges. People who are humble are grateful for the ebb and flow of life because they know that this is where they gain wisdom and strength.

As we go about the day, focusing on our thoughts, words, and actions, this will reveal to us whether we are seeking attention to boost our self-image, or if we are being humble. By integrating humility into our behavior, we will be moving closer to living an authentic life.

I

Imagination

THE HUMAN IMAGINATION IS A WONDERFUL thing. Just look around, everything you commonly use to improve the quality of your life originated in a person's imagination. No matter what it is, someone imagined it. If we can imagine it, it can be created. It may take time, but sooner or later it will come into the world.

A powerful tool for creating an authentic life would be to imagine how we want our life to look and feel. We could imagine it down to the finest detail, or we could use an open-ended thought process. Either way, if we imagine a life that is in alignment with our truth, our authentic life will come to be.

One challenge we face when using our imagination to create the life we want, is we often doubt we deserve this life. In behaving this way, we put the brakes on our intention. To create the ideal life, or any situation that will bring us joy and true happiness, we must believe it is possible.

When we use our imagination for the benefit of creating our best life possible, we may notice that things fall into place on their own. Guidance and synchronicities appear to come out of nowhere. This is because when we are being true to ourselves, the energy of our imagination attracts the necessary components for success back to us, like a magnet attracting metal.

Yet at times, our belief in our imagination may not be enough. We must do something to add energy to our dreams coming into reality. If we want to hit a game winning home run, or a hole in one at the golf course, but we do not play either sport, then we will not achieve the desired outcome.

The same is true for learning any skill, getting a raise at work, or finding the perfect life partner. We can imagine it all we want, but we must be in the right state of mind before anything positive will happen.

Some would say that using our imagination to create our best life is just daydreaming. They might even consider it a waste of time. Yet look at all the wonderful things that have been created out of a person's imagination. At one time they may have been daydreaming when a flash of inspiration caused them to act on their ideas.

Daydreaming allows us to silence our rational mind and let our thoughts wander without restrictions. A daydream can be fertile ground where we plant the seeds of an idea, thereby allowing our imagination to nurture these ideas into fruition.

The best way for our imagination to work is to clear away our self-doubt and silence our negative self-talk. These powerful sources of distraction can prevent us from living to the fullness of who we are meant to be.

Our imagination is a gift we give ourselves as we journey along the path to self-fulfillment. We must have the courage to use our imagination to create the blueprint for the life we desire.

Whatever we want to accomplish in life, we must imagine a successful outcome. We can do this by picturing ourselves in our perfect life, surrounded by all that is true for us.

At night, after I turn off the light, knowing sleep is on the way, I will imagine an opportunity I have wanted, with all the details for a successful outcome. In this short bit of time, I am in this daydream living as I have imagined. When I wake up in the morning, I have renewed energy for the work that will make my daydream a reality.

It takes little effort to imagine living to the fullness of who we are. All we have to do is believe that what we imagine is possible, as long as it aligns with our authentic self.

Inspiration

WHAT INSPIRES US? IS IT THE morning sky, the actions of others, or our desire to live a life we never thought possible? Inspiration comes in many forms, yet it will be different for each of us.

As a child I was inspired by a man who built a set of bookcases for our house. The smell and feel of the pine boards inspired me to work with wood most of my life. As an author, the eloquent words of great writers continue to inspire me to write to the best of my ability.

When we silence the chatter that clouds our focus, we will find a quiet voice within us that is always sending us messages of inspiration. This voice is the voice of our authentic self. It knows what we are capable of accomplishing and has complete faith in our capacity to succeed at whatever we set out to do.

As with anything in life, there will be times when we cannot hear our authentic voice. When this happens we may feel stuck or unmotivated. In these situations, we may seek the guidance of close, trusted friends, hoping their words will inspire us to continue our journey.

If their words resonate with us, inspiration begins to flow. But if they do not see our dreams as clearly as we do, their words may stifle our progress. In times like these we may need to seek inspiration from other sources.

One way to rekindle the flames of inspiration would be to

spend time in nature. Go for a walk in a park. If possible, find a spot next to a stream or river, or just sit quietly watching clouds roll by, focusing on their beauty.

The intention is to allow our mind to drift, without any thought of our troubles or challenges. In this quiet place, we will begin to hear the loving voice of our authentic self, encouraging us to continue following our dreams.

Oftentimes when I need inspiration, I will sit and write. Even if what I write never sees the light of day, I will have done my best to keep the flow of writing active. I may choose to write something outside my comfort zone. This is always interesting, because it inspires me to challenge myself to think and write outside the box.

We can also gain inspiration through meditation. We don't always have to sit cross legged on a cushion to meditate. We can simply close our eyes for a few minutes before we begin anything where we need inspiration. The intention is to quiet the mental chatter, allowing us to hear the voice of our true self, inspiring us to discover what is true and right for us.

When we know the truth of who we are and are courageous enough to live by this truth, we will inspire others to seek their truth. Our words and actions will serve as sources of inspiration as long as they remain true to themselves.

Intentions

THERE IS GREAT POWER IN SETTING an intention before we do anything. It can be as simple as trusting that events in life will work out for our benefit, then allowing the situations to unfold as they will. Our intention can be specific or wide in scope. Either way, learning to use the energy of our intentions will help us along our path to living an authentic life.

Some would say setting an intention is nothing but wishful thinking. If there is not a belief in the intention, then it is wishful thinking. We must believe the intention is possible, otherwise our intention will fail. In any intention there must be a true belief in success. We can say the words, but our belief will add positive energy to the intention.

It may take practice to recognize how life changing setting an intention can be, because we often set intentions without realizing it. We are constantly asking for different things in life. How often have we wished for a better outcome, a change in situation, even sunny skies for our walk? We ask for so much we often can't remember our wishes.

Imagine going to the market on a busy day. Intending the perfect parking spot, the best selection of produce, even the fastest checkout line; we must believe it's all possible. Once the intention has been set, let it go, then notice how things develop. This will tell us if our intention was heartfelt, or just wishful thinking.

When we gain confidence in our ability to set an intention, it then becomes a wonderful game of, "Let's see what we can intend now." The more joy in our intentions the better the chances of them coming to us.

Once while on my way to an appointment, I was running a little late. I intended a parking spot right next to the door of the office building. I also intended a clear road with little traffic.

After I set my intentions, I released them from my consciousness. I had set my intention, all I had to do was focus on getting to my appointment. As it turned out everything unfolded as I had intended. I even arrived a bit early to my appointment.

This may sound like a lot of hocus-pocus, but it is worth a try. We may say it's all coincidence, but is it? If we practice intending enough, we will realize it is much more than mere chance.

If our thoughts are energy, then this energy radiates out from us to the universe. Setting an intention is sending the energy of our desire out to the cosmos. One thing to realize is the energy of our thoughts and intentions act as magnets attracting back to us the essence of our intention.

We may set an intention for a table by the window at a special riverside restaurant, yet something better might happen. We may get seated next to our favorite celebrity. When we have faith in our intention something better may come along. It will all depend on the strength of our belief in the intention.

There is another aspect to intentions we should consider. It's possible to contradict our intention when we are not focused. We may want one thing, but our heart wants something else.

When this happens, nothing worthwhile will manifest, causing us to lose trust in our ability to intend successfully.

It is important to be clear about what we want before we set an intention. We may end up with something similar, but not exactly what we had originally intended. A broad intention is good, yet an intention with too many details can limit the way our intentions play out.

By practicing the skill of intending, then paying attention to the outcome, we will find just the right combination of energy for the perfect outcome. Trusting our ability to intend successfully will bring surprising results in a world that appears to be out of our control.

Intuition

FEW SOURCES OF GUIDANCE WILL BE as accurate as our own intuition. Yet how often do we tap into this powerful source of wisdom that is always sending us important messages? The challenge becomes one of understanding the meaning of these messages.

The most common type of intuitive guidance is a gut feeling. We commonly hear people say, "The situation just didn't feel right, I had a funny gut feeling." This valuable wisdom is often overlooked.

One way to know if the intuitive feeling was accurate is to notice the outcome of the situation. What happened after we made the choice to either follow the guidance, or not? The lesson will reveal itself after the experience has come to a completion.

The challenge begins when we first feel the gut feeling. We may understand what it means, yet we choose to ignore the feeling for one reason or another.

If we are in alignment with our authentic self, we will trust the feeling, thereby changing our plans. In doing so everything will flow smoothly. On the other hand, if we notice the gut feeling, recognize the message, then go forward anyway, things may not work out well for us.

I had planned a desert motorcycle ride with friends in Utah. The morning of the ride I had a strong intuitive feeling.

I understood the feeling meant, "don't go on the ride" but I went ahead anyway. As it turned out, I crashed my bike, breaking my right arm. The outcome proved to me the significance of the intuitive feeling.

It could be argued the gut feeling caused my wreck. But I have had other strong gut feelings, convincing me to change my plans and everything worked out great. I have enough experience with understanding the wisdom of a gut feeling as well as ignoring the message to know the benefits of changing my plans when I get these intuitive feelings.

Where do our intuitive feelings originate? At the core of our being is an eternal source of unconditional love. It is this love that guides us through our intuition. This never-ending flow of love has our best interest as its main focus. It is this love that will send us a gut feeling if it senses difficulty ahead. In other words, our true self loves us so much it will deliver us a message disguised as a gut feeling, advising us of the dangers ahead we may not see, or perceive.

At the foundation of our intuition is love. When we follow the wisdom of our intuition, we are self-loving. If we choose to ignore this inner guidance we have separated ourselves from this powerful source of love. When I crashed my dirt bike, I realized I didn't love myself enough to follow the guidance of my own intuition. That realization was a hard lesson to learn.

We often reserve our intuition for situations outside of everyday life, hiking, horseback riding, you name it. Situations where our health may be at risk, challenged by obvious external forces. Can we unlock our intuition to guide us throughout our daily lives?

Imagine checking in with our intuitive feelings before we begin our morning routine, our commute, parking the car, or even submitting a job application. How would things work out if we silenced the mental chatter and listened for guidance from our true self speaking through our intuition?

I have developed the habit of asking my intuition if I should take the highway, or the back way to town. Should I go to the bank, or hardware store first? These may seem like simple questions we rarely consider, yet when we are in tune with our intuition we may be saved from an unpleasant outcome.

My best advice is to give it a try, ask your intuition, then notice how things turn out. By going to the hardware store first, you may miss a fender bender in the bank parking lot. You will never know until you learn to ask your true self for guidance, then follow the wisdom of your intuition.

J

Jealousy

NOTHING WILL SEPARATE US FROM OUR authentic self quicker than jealousy. In the act of being jealous, we are saying to ourselves we would rather be someone else or have something different. Basically, we are telling ourselves that what others have, we want.

When we act this way, we block all sources of guidance leading us to exactly what we need for our best life possible. In doing so we limit our emotional and spiritual growth.

Our jealousy tells us that we will feel better about ourselves if we have a different life. Don't we realize that the life we want is at our fingertips? All we have to do is align with our truth, allowing ourselves to have all we could ever want or need.

We often associate happiness and joy with physical possessions or money. We rarely take the time to understand how things and money can burden us. Many lottery winners end up penniless after spending all their money accumulating things and buying friends. The weight of their burden is unknown to us, although we are jealous of them for what appears to be the path to an easier life.

No matter what our status in life, we have created the life we have by the thoughts we think, and the actions we take. In other words, we are responsible for the life we are currently living. In the act of being jealous of others, we are not pleased with the life we have created for ourselves.

If we are on the path to living an authentic life, then any sign of jealousy is a cue to stop and ask ourselves why we are feeling this way. It can be easy to point the finger of judgement toward those who appear to have better lives than we do. In truth, if we are judging others, we should be asking ourselves why we feel our life does not measure up to our own standards.

One way to curb our jealousy would be to learn to appreciate what we have. We may think we have little, yet if this is the case, then we should appreciate what we have no matter how small the pile. Appreciation brings us closer to living an authentic life because we realize that the things we collect do not make us who we are.

The next time we find ourselves being jealous of others, realize they could be fighting an inner battle we may know nothing about. They appear strong and centered when in public, but in private they may barely be keeping it together.

Jealousy is a form of self-judgement telling us we are not worthy of living the best life possible. We are comparing ourselves against those who have had completely different circumstances than ours. In doing so we distance ourselves from the love at the core of our being.

To live a true and authentic life, we must set aside the self-defeating emotion of jealousy. Leaving its negativity behind gives us the opportunity to move toward a place of understanding, compassion, and love. When love becomes the foundation of our thoughts, words, and behavioral patterns, we will not need jealousy to question our chosen path through life.

Joy

THERE IS A FALSE BELIEF MANY people repeat to themselves that goes, "I will be joyful when I have a better life." Placing this type of limitation on experiencing joy may keep us from living a joy filled life now. Why do we wait to experience joy?

One of the reasons we may not be living a joyous life, is because we believe the negativity swirling around in our head. Oftentimes this negative self-talk dictates our attitude, hindering our potential to experience joy.

If we are in a joyful mood, it is often short-lived, because we frequently allow the negative emotion of being overwhelmed to surface due to stresses of everyday life. This could be the reason we feel more uptight rather than joyous. Does it have to be this way?

What if we chose to be joyous before our feet hit the floor when we got out of bed? If we look closely, we will notice our emotional state of being is actually a choice we make. This may be difficult to accept but take note of how the day changes when we direct our focus toward reasons to be joyful.

We often judge the quality of our life by the things we don't have, big house, fancy cars, fast motorcycles, even a bank account filled with money. In thinking this way, we base our happiness on the accumulation of stuff. What about our health, our circle of friends, or our courage to pursue a passion; even our capacity to love another? Aren't these reasons to be filled with joy?

How often do we search for joy in the outside world, yet we fail to look within ourselves? All that stuff will wear out, lose fashion, even money can disappear. Our ability to find joy within ourselves is everlasting.

It takes little to be joyous, all we have to do is recognize how fortunate we are. Do we have food to eat, shoes to protect our feet, a roof over our head? Even if we don't have these things, we can be joyous because we can see and feel the beauty of nature.

We often think when we find joy there will be fireworks and excitement. What if joy is quiet, like the sound of a breeze through the trees, water flowing in a creek, or the voice of a lover whispering our name? Can we find joy in simple things?

Years ago, I broke my leg. After seeing the doctor, I was joyous because my leg wasn't badly broken, I would not need surgery. Seems like a crazy reason to be joyous, yet it was. Rather than becoming angry or bitter, I was relieved the injury wasn't more severe. I felt fortunate, giving me a reason to feel joy.

It may come down to the choices we make. Can we choose joy over any negative behavior? It may not be easy in many cases, but most of the time we can indeed choose joy. Instead of complaining about the line at the grocery store, we should be joyful for the ability to buy our own food.

There are two basic sides to our life experiences, one would be negative, while the other is positive. The outcome of life will be determined by the side we choose. We could be upset because it's raining, or we could remember we need water to live, causing us to be joyful for the rain.

A movement toward a positive mindset takes strength

because old patterns of behavior are hard to break. Yet, when we discover reasons to be joyful, life will shift, causing us to find more reasons to be joyous. All it takes is choosing joy as the guiding light on our journey to realizing the truth of who we are.

Judgement

O<small>F ALL THE NEGATIVE EMOTIONS, JUDGEMENT</small> seems to build quicker than any other. It's so easy to judge. We don't need a full understanding of the situation, or the people involved, we just judge, oftentimes without much thought.

Yet if our intention is to live to the fullness of who we are, we must recognize the reasons we judge so quickly. Do we judge because we need to feel superior to others? Are we convinced we are right while everyone else is wrong? Thereby judging others harshly? Does our judgement make us feel better about ourselves, boosting our fragile ego?

We often judge with little accurate information. It is important to remember that no one truly knows what another person has, or is, going through emotionally. Yet our judgement of them is often presented as fact, even though we know little about their challenges.

As we walk the path to an authentic life, we will learn that everyone is doing the best they can. Our judgement is often based on a desire for others to behave in a way that pleases us. When they don't, our judgement may be quick and severe.

If we ask others to act in a certain way, we do so because we believe their behavior will make us happy. In this way, our happiness is attached to their actions. But we fail to realize that their behavior now controls us emotionally. This is an unhealthy way to go through life because we will always be judging people based on how well they have changed who they are to make us happy.

At some level, judgement makes us feel better about ourselves. It has nothing to do with helping those we judge to improve. We use their perceived shortcomings as a measure of our self-worth. It seems that no matter what others do we will judge them, because we don't love ourselves enough to accept that everyone is doing their best.

Oftentimes our judgement of others prevents us from knowing the truth of a person. We judge on a superficial level, without taking the time and energy to understand why people are the way they are. It has become too easy to judge, preventing us from taking the time to learn and understand what difficulties a person has experienced.

The path to higher levels of consciousness is a journey up the emotional scale. Each emotion we experience radiates energy. Love is at the top of the scale, while hate is at the very bottom. Judgement is a powerful negative emotion found on the lower end of the scale.

To reach higher levels of awareness and discover our authentic self, we must work our way up this scale. Thereby moving away from the energy of negativity, toward the positive energy of kindness, compassion, and love.

This means that to live a truly authentic life, founded on unconditional love, we must set aside our need to judge others as well as ourselves. This shift in awareness will open our heart to the world around us without the negativity of judgement.

The best we can do for ourselves and those in our life, is to become aware of the first hint of judgement. When we notice this negative emotion building in strength, we can quickly shut it down by accepting that everyone is doing their best.

It's also good to remember that those who we judge may be fighting an inner battle we know nothing about. When we accept this powerful truth, our need to judge falls away. In our state of acceptance, the love at the core of our being becomes the driving force in our lives. This is where we begin to live an authentic life, a life founded on gratitude, understanding, and love.

Jump

To ACHIEVE ANYTHING WORTHWHILE IN LIFE, we must take a leap of faith. In other words, to be successful we must jump.

Our comfort zone is not our friend. Although it may make us feel warm and cozy now, we might regret it in the future. How often do we have a list of great ideas, only to set them aside because accomplishing them means we must jump into the unknown?

Have we surrounded ourselves with people who take leaps of faith? Those who are living a life of purpose, in making these choices, have they discovered their authentic selves? Or are we hanging out with those who are living in their comfort zone? Motivational speaker, Jim Rohn said, "You're the average of the five people you spend the most time with."

Thinking of this quote causes us to look at our circle of friends. Are they comfortable in their lives? Or have they jumped, seeking new opportunities, growing from the possibilities? Have they learned some hard -fought lessons?

Life can be as exciting or as comfortable as we choose to make it. The choice is always ours. We can choose to remain on the couch of life, or we can challenge ourselves with the intention of seeing how far we can go.

Taking a leap of faith is jumping into the unknown. Although if we have learned to trust our intuition, we then have the wisdom and guidance to lead us along our journey.

Trusting our intuitive feelings will make our leap of faith less frightening.

If we were to jump on a trampoline, we would notice we gain more height than the energy we put into our jump. Life works the same way. When our intention is to live to the fullness of who we are, life will help us move forward on our journey.

By being courageous enough to jump, the right people will come into our lives at the right time. We will notice more synchronicities and coincidences. Opportunities and guidance will appear out of nowhere. This is the bounce effect of jumping into your authentic self.

The challenge is knowing when to jump and when to keep our feet firmly planted. Not all possibilities are meant for our exploration. We must learn to recognize what has meaning for us, and those things that do not. There will be important lessons for our growth either way.

One thing to expect when we jump will be the growth that comes from our leap of faith. We often jump into the unknown, but if we are aware, we will be open to the lessons needed for our success.

How will we know if we are jumping for the right reasons? As with any leap of faith, we must learn to trust our intuition before our feet leave the ground. This will give us the insights needed to know if we are moving in the right direction, or leaping for a goal that has true meaning and purpose.

It is possible we could leap, and things don't work out. If so, there will always be lessons hidden within these experiences. When circumstances don't go as planned, look for the positive lessons then use this wisdom to better prepare before we jump again.

It can be frightening to leave our comfort zone and jump into the unfamiliar. Yet if we learn to trust ourselves, and follow the wisdom of our inner guidance, we will float gently to the ground, because we will have grown wings of confidence along the way.

Karma

At some point in life we've heard the word and may have experienced some form of karma. Throughout the spiritual teachings of the world, there are many nuances regarding karma. For convenience, "cause and effect" will be the basis for our conversation.

We may think we are immune from the fallout of our actions, although have we stopped to notice how our life is unfolding? To recognize karma in action, we must take the time to look back on life, to become aware of the impact of our behavior.

The interesting thing about karma is it makes no difference if we are kind or nasty. At some point the result of our actions will be revealed to us. Kindness will be returned as kindness, while being nasty will return nastiness to us. It's an easy concept to grasp when we are kind, a bit more difficult to comprehend when we are nasty.

This is where finding the courage to self-examine our behavior benefits our emotional growth. If life hands us a challenging person who makes us unhappy, our questions could be, "Why is this person in our life?" Or, "How did we behave in the past to deserve this treatment?" It takes stamina to review our past behavior to find the answers to these questions. Remember, being honest with ourselves is the foundation to living an authentic life.

The key with people who make life difficult, is how we react to their behavior. Karma says, "What goes around, comes around." Our reaction to those who treat us poorly will come back to either haunt us or move us forward in a positive direction. It takes a truthful evaluation of our actions and the outcome, to recognize the karmic lessons.

One way to understand karma better is to imagine our life force energy as powerful magnets, attracting back to us the essence of the energy we radiate. If we express love, kindness, and compassion to others, karma will return similar energy to us. On the other hand, if we are rude, resentful, or vindictive, karma says we will attract the same level of energy into our life.

In a way, karma is a great indicator of past behavior. We must be truthful with ourselves when making the connection between what we are going through now and our actions of the past. It can be easy to blame others for the outcome of our life, yet our behavior may be the root cause of any discomfort we may be experiencing.

Karma teaches us to be kind to those who are unkind, pleasant to the grumpy, and loving to those who for one reason or another, seem to be unlovable. Karma also teaches us that at any moment our life could be turned upside down. We could suddenly find ourselves without a job, homeless, or alone. How we treat others now determines how life will treat us in the future.

As we walk the path to reconnect with our authentic self, we can use karma as a tool to reawaken our inner truth. If surprising coincidences occur, and supportive people appear, we will know our past behavior was in alignment with our true self. If on the other hand life is full of unexpected obstacles and difficult people continually show up, it might be time to reevaluate our behavior.

We may consider karma a reflection of what is in our heart. When we walk the path of honesty and love, our karma will align with this truth. But if we are not living a truthful, love-filled life, karma will expose our weaknesses. As we learn lessons from our karmic experiences, we elevate our consciousness. Thereby helping us live in harmony with our authentic self.

Keys

I DROPPED MY KEY RING THE other day. While picking it up I noticed their different shapes and sizes. One thing that stood out was each key went to a certain lock, and no two keys opened the same lock.

What if we were to consider that to live to the fullness of who we are, we must unlock the chains that hinder our forward progress? We often spend much of our life searching outside of ourselves for these keys. We think our life partner is the special key. Even our new job, or location could be the key we're searching for. Yet it doesn't always work out as we had hoped.

At some level these keys will unlock certain doors. But the key that will allow us to go further than we could possibly imagine will be found deep within us. This key is often buried beneath our self-doubt, negative self-talk, and the limiting beliefs we have come to accept as true. The problem with finding this key is having the courage to challenge many of the negative thoughts we have about ourselves.

The work of looking within ourselves and clearing away the thoughts and beliefs that limit our true potential can be overwhelming. We have created a life based on our thoughts, so questioning them can shake us emotionally. If we have constructed a life based on thoughts and beliefs that are not true and right for us, what kind of life have we built?

If our intention is to live a true and authentic life, we must be willing to do the inner work to uncover the truth of who we are. One way to begin this work is to accept that at any given moment we are doing the best we can. This may seem like an easy way out, but we often judge ourselves harshly for the slightest misstep. Knowing we are always doing our best is a key that opens a door to realizing our authentic self.

Judging ourselves based on the unrealistic standards of society is one way we hinder our ability to experience our authentic truth. At some level we believe we should behave in a certain way, act a certain way, and speak a certain way, to be accepted by others. Even if our actions do not align with our truth, we think this is the path to being authentic. But how does this make us feel?

As we allow the belief that we are always doing the best we can to fill our consciousness, we unlock the door to our own powerful self-love. This love has no need to judge us or others. It is a source of unconditional love so strong, that when we allow this love to fill our being, our negative self-talk and self-doubt are silenced, allowing us to see our limiting beliefs as opportunities for emotional growth. The possibilities are end-less when we unlock our potential supported by our self-love.

It is not only us who benefit from realizing our self-love. Those we encounter each and every day will feel the difference in us as we move away from the negativity of judgement toward the loving space of acceptance.

Our words, thoughts, and actions now have a foundation rooted in unconditional love. All because we chose to do the inner work to find the right key, which opens the door, leading us toward our authentic self.

Kindness

THE MEASURE OF A PERSON'S KINDNESS is gauged by how they treat those who can do nothing for them. Yet expressing kindness is the easiest way to share the love found at the core of our being.

Why is speaking and behaving in kindness so difficult? Do we believe it is a sign of weakness? How can that be? I would think being kind is a sign of strength. Living a fulfilling life means we are strong enough in our self-love to share our kindness freely, without the expectation of a reward.

As we begin the journey of uncovering our authentic self, we arrive at a place of unconditional love. This love has no limits, boundaries, or expectations. It is a free-flowing source of eternal love. One of the ways we express this love is through acts of kindness.

We often think our generosity must be big and grand to have a lasting impact. This false belief may prevent us from simple acts of kindness. If we use the analogy of tossing a pebble in a pond, we notice how the ripples spread out across the pond affecting everything above and below the water. Sharing our kindness works the same way.

No matter how small our acts of kindness may appear, they do indeed have a positive effect on the world around us. The difficulty begins when we expect a reward for our behavior. It is this expectation that takes the love out of the kindness. To give our kindness freely is a true act of love.

Yet many people are not in tune with the unlimited source of love found within their authentic self. They are too involved with themselves to share their love. Could it be they believe love is finite, or in short supply? One thing to remember is nothing grows more love than to express love freely. In other words, the more love we give away, the more love we will experience.

True kindness is not to be rationed to only those with whom we agree. There must be no hesitation if we assume ourselves to be kind. The love of our true self loves all, not just a chosen few.

At times being kind can be difficult. The world can be a challenging place, with many struggles to overcome. Yet kindness helps soften the edges that arise when we have been hardened by life.

Our kindness reflects who we are, the beliefs we hold, and the depth of love in our heart. We may never know how a simple act of kindness might change a person's life. The ripple effect of our kindness goes unseen. Although this should not stop us from being kind to those who can do nothing for us.

Knowing

THINK OF A TIME WHEN YOU knew something was true and right, without question. You didn't know why you knew it, but you didn't doubt it, you just knew it. Where does this "knowing" originate? It may be hard to describe to those who have never experienced this kind of feeling. At times it may be difficult to describe ourselves.

A sense of knowing is our connection with the eternal wisdom found at the core of our being. We know it is authentic because it resonates deep within us. We understand this knowing as the truth.

Yet we often doubt this knowing because we, as humans, want to see proof it exists before we believe it to be true. Searching for evidence of this truth limits the way we experience this knowing. If we doubt it exists, we will see reasons justifying our doubt, thereby limiting access to our sense of knowing.

When we seek proof of anything we cannot explain, we block the very information needed to validate its existence. We must learn to trust a feeling. Yet knowing goes deeper than a feeling. If we are attuned to knowing, we feel stable, solid, confident. If our world shakes, we will be safe, we trust the guidance woven within the knowing.

For some reason we ignore the wisdom of our knowing because it may be contrary to what we have been taught. Much of our life is spent adjusting to the beliefs of others. Looking within ourselves for the answers we cannot find in the physical world may be new to us. If we are always searching outside of ourselves for guidance, we limit our ability to access higher realms of consciousness found in our knowing.

What if our knowing is a reunion with the truth of who we are? Imagine having infinite knowledge along with unlimited insights when we came into this world at birth. Yet through time, this wisdom and understanding have been buried beneath the frantic pace of life. With each new experience, we became addicted to the stimulation found in the physical world. Wanting to see and feel more, we moved away from our sense of knowing toward a life of instant gratification.

If our intention is to live to the fullness of who we are, we must work our way back to our knowing. Finding quiet time through meditation is a way to reconnect with the wisdom we are seeking. Having the emotional strength to ignore our thoughts, while working to quiet the mind and body, will allow the pathways of our knowing to flow once again.

The challenge becomes one of differentiating our knowing from the noise circulating in our head. Any thought not founded on love, kindness, and compassion, is not a true knowing. The wisdom of our knowing is rather simple, yet at times difficult to accept.

It's realizing that deep within us is a source of unconditional love guiding us through life. Each of us has this love at the core of our being. Some are aware of this love, while others are separated from this knowing. To live a complete and authentic life we must accept the wisdom this love teaches.

Our knowing is a higher state of consciousness available to us when we align with our inner source of love. We know it to be true because we will have no doubt or hesitation when surrounded by the warmth of this energy.

As we learn to trust the truth of this love, the wisdom of our knowing will guide us through life. Any question can be asked, and loving guidance will answer. All that is asked of us is to trust the truth of our knowing.

Labels

WHAT LABELS DO WE PLACE ON others? Do our labels reflect the truth of who these people are? Or are these labels filled with misinformation and judgement? Labeling is easy, it takes no thought. While many times they lack truth, we choose labels anyway.

It seems we believe everyone needs a label. In some way, labels make us comfortable. When we categorize a person or a group of people, our label defines them. But is our label accurate?

When we ship a package, we place a label on the box. In a sense, we do the same when we label people, we place them in a box. The characterization of who we think they are is now found in a box with a label.

In our need to label others, we fail to realize we are doing so to control our discomfort. If we can't understand them, or their lifestyle makes us uneasy, we label them to justify our opinion of them. That's the issue, isn't it? We are not accepting of those who live life differently.

What would happen if instead of labeling others, we allowed ourselves the ability to recognize the unique authenticity found in all people? It might be difficult at first because we must work through the preconceived ideas that created the labels. Once we move past these limiting beliefs, we will begin to see the truth of the person or group of people.

Oftentimes our labels are projections of the biases we hold toward others. We may not know the origins of our prejudice, yet we can work through these biases if we are willing to question the reasons we label.

Think of a time when someone placed a label on us. How did it make us feel? Did we notice the judgement and falsehoods in the label? If we have been labeled, there may not have been any true knowledge of who we are.

Consider the labels we assign to those we don't understand. Is there any benefit in our label? What is the root cause of our behavior? Is it possible to let go of our need to label while we work to become more tolerant?

Living an authentic life means we have no need to put people in a box with a label defining them. We love ourselves enough to accept people for who they are, even though we may not understand them.

At the core of our being is an eternal source of unconditional love. This love teaches us to walk through life without the impulse to label or judge anyone. If we do not understand others or their lifestyle, we are courageous enough to seek answers. With knowledge comes an opportunity for clarity and acceptance.

It is not only others we label. We also label ourselves. Think of the words we use to describe ourselves to others. Are these words kind and generous? What words do we use when we make a mistake at work, or stub a toe?

Words have power beyond their physical meaning. When we label, we add energy to these words through the intention we place on the word. If for some reason we call ourselves "dumb or stupid" for forgetting an appointment, we label ourselves as not very smart. It may not seem like much, but it is. At a level deep within our consciousness, we hear these negative words thereby creating a self-image based on these labels.

Although labeling may be fun, boosting our worth with others, we do harm to ourselves and those we label. To live to the fullness of who we are, we must explore why we act this way, then clear this need from our awareness. Once we arrive at an emotional state of acceptance and tolerance, our journey to uncover our authentic self will have one less obstacle to overcome.

Limitations

Have we ever stopped to listen to the words we say to ourselves? Are these words supportive and kind? Or are we repeating words that limit the way we experience life?

Many of our limitations begin with what we say to ourselves. If we say, "We can't." Guess what? We won't. Yes, of course we will face obstacles in life, yet many of our limitations are self-imposed.

Our limiting beliefs often begin with what we were taught when we were children. At a young age we trusted the words of those around us. They claimed to love us, so we believed they would only speak the truth. We used their words to create a belief system about ourselves. As children we had no point of reference to gauge if their words were true or not.

Another source of limiting beliefs would be a history of failed attempts. We often think if we could not do it then, we can't do it now. Oftentimes we allow these failures to define who we are, thereby limiting our ability to live to our potential.

Of course, there will be physical limitations we may not be able to overcome. Yet we can challenge our physical body to see how far we can go. Many ultra-marathon athletes speak of the body having the resilience to go the distance, but it is the mind that wants to quit. In other words, our body may be able to overcome physical barriers, it's our mind that's the weak link.

As we think of this, many of our beliefs come from our mind. We believe what the mind says, even if it is arguing for our limitations. We tell ourselves this negative conversation must be true because our mind knows us so well. If we can control the mental chatter, we have power over the outcome.

Most of our beliefs have been created by past experiences. The mind is only reminding us of these failures. When we shift focus away from our negative self-talk and self-doubt, we begin to hear the voice of our true self. We know this voice is authentic because it only speaks words of encouragement and love. Any other voice we hear in our head should be ignored.

While contemplating our limitations we must consider our circle of associates. Are they supportive, encouraging us to go for it? Or are they themselves living a life bound by limitations? If we challenge ourselves with the intention of realizing our full potential, we may make those in our circle uncomfortable. They may choose not to support us because they don't want to be left behind.

Yet to live to the fullness of who we are meant to be, we must shed the limitations that keep us from moving forward emotionally, even if these changes cause us to lose friends. We will never regret being truthful to ourselves, although we may regret remaining small to please others.

If we are hesitant about moving forward, we can look to history or social media to find those who have pushed through their challenges to become successful. Their stories will be different than ours, but they may inspire us to silence the self-doubting chatter flooding our mind.

When we begin to question our limitations, we notice they are hollow beliefs we thought were made of solid stone. There is little truth in many of our false beliefs, yet they appear true because we have been repeating these beliefs to ourselves for years.

By challenging our limiting beliefs, we gain strength and courage to continue moving forward. The more we do this, the more self-confidence we gain. It then becomes easier to question many other beliefs obstructing our progress.

We often think of limitations as our inability to climb the world's tallest mountains, or our fear of jumping out of a perfectly good airplane. We fail to question the limitations keeping us from pursuing our dreams. Even if the dream is to play a musical instrument, or create art. Our limiting beliefs prevent us from living to the fullness of who we are.

One question we could ask ourselves would be, "Don't we love ourselves enough to see what we are capable of accomplishing?" If we accept our limitations as how the world works, we are hindering the way we love ourselves.

If our intention is to live authentically, it is essential to question our limitations. This opens the door to unseen possibilities, giving us the opportunity to experience our true self, while we contemplate our future from a new perspective.

Listen

THERE IS MUCH TO HEAR IN life, but do we listen? We could say listening is hearing on a more conscious level. To listen well, we must set aside our predetermined ideas of how we want things to unfold. We must become aware of the nuances within the messages we hear. This only happens when we listen.

It is true, a lot of noise bombards us every day. Although within the noise are the messages we are meant to receive, yet we must silence the chatter and listen. It may seem odd there are messages in the noise, but if we listen carefully, we will hear what we need to hear.

Once I was pondering a choice when I heard someone shout, "No!" I took this as a sign and declined the offer. Seems crazy, yet as it turned out by making this choice, I allowed a better opportunity to enter my life. I had asked for guidance and was listening for an answer. As I have since learned, guidance flows in many different ways.

The thing is, we must be listening to hear the guidance. How often do we ask for guidance, but never hear it? It could be we are too busy asking and not centered enough to listen for the wisdom.

Our intuition is always speaking to us, although we may not be in tune with hearing the voice of our inner truth. As we learn to silence our mental chatter and listen for our inner voice, our life will change because our intuition is always looking out for our best interests.

At times our inner voice will speak to us as a gut feeling, other times it might be a subtle pressure, urging us in a certain direction. It may even be a billboard telling us to go for it. Yet we must be listening for the answers we are seeking.

It can be difficult to hear the messages we are meant to hear. Our self-doubt and negative self-talk are such loud voices, oftentimes shouting negativity at a level making it hard to concentrate or think clearly. Having the courage to silence these two voices will give us the stillness needed to hear the words of our authentic self.

One of the challenges we often face with the voices we hear in our head is knowing which voice is the one we should believe and trust. I've made a habit of following the voice that speaks only through love. If the guidance is founded on love, then this is the voice I will follow.

It takes practice knowing the value of the messages we receive. For one reason or another we may choose to go in a different direction than the guidance suggests. The only way to know if we did the right thing is to notice the outcome. How things unfold will reveal to us if we were listening to our inner voice or ignoring this important information.

Listening to the voice of our authentic self may not be easy. The outside world is constantly trying to tell us what to think, how to behave, and who to believe. There is little encouragement to follow the wisdom of our intuition. But when we silence the nonsense in our head, we will have the ability to listen for the loving voice of our authentic self.

Love

Tragically, the word "love" has become overused to a point where it has lost much of its original meaning. Overused because we have attached the word love to everything from our car to our favorite style of pizza. With so much use, at times the word has little significance.

When we begin to look past the superficial use of the word love, we realize love is the root of all true happiness. Yet it goes deeper than that. Love is the driving force of our authentic self.

If we are honest with ourselves, living to the fullness of who we are, we must love ourselves without judgements, conditions, or limitations. That's the challenge, isn't it? Can we look in the mirror and love who we see no matter what difficulties we are facing in life?

Is it possible to love ourselves when we are struggling in life? What would happen if we loved ourselves so much, a challenging period would be seen as an opportunity to grow stronger emotionally, a path to loving ourselves more deeply?

Rather than berate ourselves for making a mistake, can we recognize the lessons in the experience? Then move on, while accepting we were doing the best we could, given what we knew at the time?

It doesn't take much to notice the reasons we may not love ourselves. Our negative self-talk is always putting us down. Our self-doubt never stops hindering the way we experience life. Then we have our limiting beliefs, those taught to us by people who claimed to love us. These are the most difficult to overcome because we may have been hearing these types of messages from an early age.

If our intention is to live an authentic life, it is essential to begin the work of discovering the love found at the core of our being. As we learn to silence the mental chatter in our head, we will hear the voice of our true self. This is the voice of our intuition. Founded on love, the purpose of our intuition is to guide us to a life filled with joy, happiness, and love.

When we align with the truth of our self-love, we connect with the courage needed to shift our life in a way that brings true meaning. Not a life that is adequate, but a life that surpasses our wildest expectations.

In this state of love, we love others without asking them to change who they are to please us. That's the thing about true love, we love without conditions or expectations. We cannot love others only when their behavior makes us happy. We must love them even if we feel betrayed. To love deeply is to be honest with ourselves while forgiving others for their transgressions. Loving halfway is not true love.

Imagine an eternal source of love flowing through our body. This love causes our heart to beat, our lungs to inhale and exhale, our body to heal. It also shows us the way through the inner guidance of our intuition and gut feelings. This love allows us to realize the truth of who we are, then gives us the strength to live by this truth.

How do we know if we are living by the power of our inner source of love? Listen to the words we use to describe ourselves and others. Are these words positive, kind, and compassionate?

Or do we judge without thought, or consideration for the difficulties others have faced in life?

Our words broadcast the thoughts we think about the world around us. They often reveal if we are being honest with ourselves. They will also show people who we are, whether we have accessed the love in our heart or not.

Using the word love is easy, giving it genuine meaning is a bit more difficult. Yet if we want to live a truthful life, we must connect with the love at the core of our being. Otherwise, we are underestimating the power of a word that has the ability to deliver to us the truth of who we are.

Mirror

IMAGINE IF EVERY WORD WE SPOKE, or action we took, was reflected back to us by a giant mirror? Thereby giving us an opportunity to see how our behavior affects others. Think of it as watching a reflection of our behavior as life unfolds before our very eyes. Would we be pleased, or shocked by what we see?

I often wonder if people understand how their behavior affects those they encounter as they go about their day. As I take an honest look back at my life, I shudder at how I sometimes acted and treated others, having little self-awareness to notice how I behaved.

It may not be easy seeing our life reflected back to us, but if we are honest with ourselves, we can learn from these experiences. Life is funny because we are often given a test, then taught the lesson. If we think of a giant mirror following us around all day, we will have an opportunity to notice if we are acting through kindness, compassion, and love, or not. Seeing our behavior this way gives us a chance to learn from our actions.

We often don't want to examine our behavior because it may cause us some discomfort. We justify our actions for one reason or another. Although if we find reasons to defend our negative behavior, we will not see a clear path to living a healthier way of life.

The past is gone, there is nothing we can do about it. Yet

if we are courageous, we can take an honest look at why we behaved as we did, then search for the reasons behind our actions. Once we recognize the root cause of our behavior, we can begin the healing process, working to eliminate these unhealthy emotional traits from our consciousness.

As we shed these patterns from our awareness, we'll notice we are doing the best we can. Along with the reflection of us going through the day, we will also see the emotional struggles we may be facing. This will help us forgive ourselves for not being in alignment with our authentic self.

Once we forgive ourselves, we begin the self-loving task of taking responsibility for our actions. This requires us to accept that the mirror does not lie. What we see in our reflection is indeed a true representation of who we show to the world.

Yet, the who we share with those around us may not be the truth of who we are. Oftentimes we create a persona to protect ourselves from the pain the world may inflict on us. Who we see in the mirror may not be who we are, but a façade we have created as a way to control that which cannot be controlled.

As difficult as it may be to look into this mirror, we must if our desire is to move away from our limiting behavior, toward a life of honesty and truth. The future is before us, yet we can learn much from the past, if we are strong enough to contemplate what we see reflected in the mirror.

Mistakes

I WOULD LIKE TO SAY I have never made a mistake in my life, but that's not possible. To live life is to make mistakes. Yet do we consider our mistakes opportunities for learning and growth?

Life is interesting because we are often taught the lesson after we make the mistake. To see the lessons in our mistakes is to grow from the experience. Oftentimes we are too busy blaming others or criticizing ourselves, for the way things turned out, that we fail to learn anything.

It takes courage and an honest desire to grow emotionally to understand the lessons found in our mistakes. We must go through the effort of self-examination before we can arrive at the heart of the lesson.

This can be challenging because we have to take responsibility for the way our life unfolds, no matter the outcome. It is much easier to avoid accountability by blaming circumstances outside of our control, than it is to accept our role in the mistake.

One thing that limits our ability to learn from our mistakes is we often judge ourselves harshly because we made a mistake. This behavior prevents us from having the awareness to see the hidden lessons within those mistakes.

What would happen if we judged ourselves on the positive things we learned from our mistakes? This would make us feel better about ourselves, allowing us to heal quicker emotionally than if we were to dwell on our shortcomings.

Mistakes give us an opportunity to see what we need to learn to become more connected with our authentic self. This may be a tough way to discover who we are, but we will benefit from these challenges.

Some of our mistakes may have painful outcomes. That's the nature of being human. Yet when we do our best to search out the lessons these mistakes hold for us, we will begin the healing process. In time we may begin to appreciate the growth we experience from these situations.

A continued focus on our mistakes will keep us from moving forward emotionally. In a way, we are stuck because we can't seem to get past the mistake. This is where self-forgiveness will set us free from the shackles of overthinking our actions.

We can forgive ourselves by accepting that we are always doing the best we can, no matter what the situation. If we make a mistake, we should forgive ourselves, search for the positive lesson, then move on.

There is no point in carrying a mistake through life. Self-forgiveness will help us let it go. This will enable us to return to a place of self-love, thereby allowing us to connect with our emotional center, our place of truth and authenticity.

Monsters

WHEN WE WERE CHILDREN, WE WERE afraid of the monsters we imagined hiding under the bed. As years passed, we realized nothing lived there; for a while we felt safe. In time, we noticed that the monsters still come out at night...only now they reside in our head.

Why is it nighttime can be so difficult? Is it because the busyness of the physical world has stopped, and there is nothing to keep our attention away from the voices we hear in our head?

Do we become overwhelmed by the force of our self-doubt, or the condescending tone of our negative self-talk? Is it possible we tell ourselves our life is unfulfilled because of the limiting beliefs we think are true?

Monsters come in many shapes and forms. I often lay awake because of the regret from the should'a, would'a, could'a's in my life. Although there is little I can do about the past, for some reason this monster keeps me awake.

The interesting thing about our hectic world is we have become too shy to reveal our monsters to others. Each of us wants to appear strong to those around us, yet in doing so we give our monsters a safe place to hide. The longer we harbor these villains, the more power they seem to have over our well-being.

Our monsters grow in strength because of the almost constant diet of negative self-talk, self-doubt, and false beliefs we feed them throughout the day. Although much negativity can come from the outside world, we must pay attention to how we reinforce the negativity swirling around in our head.

The voice of this doom and gloom seems to be the loudest in the middle of the night, forcing us to lay there, eyes wide open, with no chance of falling into a blissful sleep. For some reason in the darkness, we are not strong enough to slay these beasts.

A method to disarm monsters would be to create a gratitude list before going to bed. The intention is to write everything for which we are grateful in a journal. This shifts our mind away from the struggles we may have faced during the day, toward the things that bring us feelings of joy and happiness.

At first it may be difficult to come up with reasons to be grateful, but even one reason might be enough to keep the monsters at bay. Once we finish the list, focus on what has been written. In doing so, our energy will change, becoming more positive, allowing us the opportunity to get some rest.

Making a gratitude list is not just limited to bedtime. Anytime we feel the monsters getting the upper hand, create a list. If we can't stop to write, recite the list. In doing so we give ourselves permission to raise our emotional state of mind away from the lower levels of energy where monsters live.

We often forget that at the core of our being is a source of unconditional love. As we begin the journey of discovering the truth of who we are, we gain access to this love. Our self-love is the antidote for monsters. The more we love ourselves the more fearful our monsters will be of us.

With each new gratitude list, our self-love deepens, lifting us to higher levels of consciousness. In this elevated awareness our monsters will be too afraid to show themselves. We love ourselves enough so when monsters do arrive, they will not have the strength to disrupt our inner peace.

That's all because we love ourselves enough to learn the truth of who we are, thereby giving us the courage to silence our negative self-talk, ignoring our self-doubt. We will know that any belief not founded in love is a belief worth releasing from our consciousness. Yes, at times monsters may surface, yet it will be the depth of the love for ourselves that will defeat them.

Motivation

W<small>HAT MOTIVATES US TO DO GREAT</small> things? Is it the sight of a beautiful piece of art, or hearing pleasing music? Do we find inspiration in the behavior of others, thus motivating us to run a marathon, or step out of our comfort zone in some way?

The simplest things can motivate us, yet these same sources of motivation can overwhelm us, stopping us in our tracks. One reason may be because we often focus on the finished product and not on the steps needed to accomplish the goal.

To be successful at anything takes many small steps. These steps have an order that when combined, create a completed goal. When writing a book each word has to be written. To carve a statue out of marble, small chips must be removed from the stone. Any worthy piece of music begins with an idea, then individual notes must be written down.

Each step along the way to success can inspire us to continue or can defeat us. It will depend on how motivated we are. I have seen many talented craftsmen accomplish very little in their career. They didn't have the motivation to challenge themselves.

As with much of life, we will have days where we accomplish a lot, then we may have other days when getting out of bed is challenging. It comes down to the amount of motivation we have within us at the time.

Our desire to live the best life possible will be determined by how well we focus on living the best life possible. It's easy to talk about it on social media, but it can be much harder to do the work needed to succeed at this goal.

To run a marathon, we must get off the couch and run. To write books we must sit and write. This can be easy at first, but when distractions arise do we have the discipline to put on our running shoes or sit and type word after word?

If we are aligned with our true purpose, the act of living this purpose will be the fuel we need to keep moving forward each and every day. In a way, living our truth is the motivation we need to get up and continue pushing through any distractions that may appear before us.

The internet is a wonderful tool, yet it can also be a drain on our time. Social media is a great way to share our progress, but it can also be a source of discouragement when we compare ourselves to others in our respective fields.

By taking a closer look at motivation we will discover it has a root in self-love. We love ourselves enough to remain focused on what brings us true joy and happiness, thereby giving us the strength to keep moving forward toward our goals. Even if the goal is to be a better person today than we were yesterday.

Motivation is not reserved for artists or poets. Anyone who wants to improve their life in some way will need motivation to keep going when times get tough. The attraction of doing anything other than the hard work needed for an inspired life can be strong when life becomes challenging.

The days when we feel unmotivated are the most important days to get up and do the work. Why? It is these days when we discover how dedicated we are to our dreams. No one is going to write for me. No one is going to paint or run for you. It's all up to us.

The interesting thing about doing our work on the days we don't feel motivated is before we know it, on a deep inner level we notice the thrill of doing what aligns with our truth. It may be hard, it may not come easy, but it will be worth it in the long run.

We might even struggle with producing anything worthwhile. Or, we may work through an emotional block that has been hindering us for some time. This will give us a better feeling about ourselves than if we had given up for the day and remained in bed.

Each of us has an unlimited source of motivation. All we have to do to access this energy is to silence our negative self-talk and ignore our self-doubt. Our source of motivation will be found deep within us. If we want to live by the truth of who we are, we must allow our inner motivation the freedom to propel us throughout the day, one step at a time.

N

Narrative

THE STORIES WE TELL OURSELVES CREATE our life experience. Yet how often do we stop to examine what we say to ourselves? Are these stories negative or positive? If we are repeating a negative narrative, do we realize we are building a life supported by these stories? If our narrative is positive, how is life unfolding?

The interesting thing about life is we establish our reality based on what we believe, the words we speak, and the actions we take. If our narrative is positive and uplifting, then our life will reflect this. On the other hand, if our thoughts, words, and behavior, are negative, we will create an environment that has negativity as its foundation.

If we want to understand our narrative, we need to take an honest look at how we interact with the world around us. The outside world will reflect the inner world we create through the stories we repeat to ourselves.

To live an authentic life, we must admit that our narrative is being reinforced every moment of every day by what we tell ourselves. Positive or negative, we are creating our life by the thoughts we think, the words we speak, and the actions we take. Questioning our narrative with the intention of seeking a healthier life is the path to uncovering the truth of who we are.

If we want to live to our full potential, we must clear away the thoughts and beliefs that do not serve our greater good. Any belief or thought not founded on love should be questioned to see if it adds value to our life. If not, it must be released from our consciousness. Thereby setting us free from the limitations the false belief has placed on us.

It can be difficult to question the very thoughts and beliefs that have created the life we live. But if these thoughts and beliefs are negative, they will hinder the way we experience the world. Our narrative shapes who we are. If we choose to challenge the stories we repeat to ourselves, there is the possibility this could shake our foundation to its core.

One way to begin changing our negative narrative is to accept that at the depths of our being is a source of unconditional love. It is this love that will guide us throughout our day if we can silence our negative mental chatter.

A negative narrative will prevent us from trusting ourselves, because we think this is the voice of our authentic self. The constant low-level energy of negativity will drain us emotionally, causing us to feel tired or rundown. When this happens, it may be time to examine our thoughts, words, and actions.

The more we repeat our narrative the stronger it will become. If we continue this behavior, the strength of our narrative may be too difficult to overcome. Because of this we often create an identity based on the stories we tell ourselves. We find comfort in them, so there is little reason to question these stories. In living this way, we separate ourselves from the truth of who we are.

When we begin to focus on the love at the core of our being, our stories will shift away from our limiting beliefs toward a life with endless possibilities. Yet we must be courageous enough to question our narrative. Only then will we realize we have the power to create an authentic life.

Needs

Each of us has basic needs: companionship, healthy food, clean water to drink, and a safe place to live. These needs are universal to all walks of life. When these needs are satisfied, we are at peace. If we are searching for ways to fulfill these needs, we may feel lost, or emotionally unsettled.

Some needs are beneficial to our physical and spiritual health, while others do not align with our authentic truth. Needs can range from eating well, to working at being a better person, to remaining centered when life challenges us. Yet our needs can also hinder our ability to live truthfully.

If we look deeper into our needs, we may notice a need for others to conduct themselves in a way that pleases us. We might not think this is a need, yet when they behave poorly, our emotional stability crumbles. We believe if they acted better, we would be happy.

The interesting thing about this need is we allow others to control us. If they do please us, we believe we are in control. If they don't, our life is a storm of negative emotions.

When this happens, we often blame them for disrupting our serenity, believing it's their fault we are upset or angry. We take no responsibility for maintaining our own peace of mind if we respond to their actions this way.

If we get angry at others because they upset us, we have allowed them to control us emotionally. At the root of our need for others to please us, is a lack of self-love. We could deny this, yet if we loved ourselves, their behavior would not bother us. This may seem odd, but when we love ourselves, we constantly reinforce our need to keep ourselves emotionally balanced.

As we strengthen our need to reconnect with our self-love, we notice those who anger us may be separated from their own eternal source of love. Our self-love teaches us to understand that their behavior reflects the emotional challenges hidden within them.

Oftentimes we have a need to blame others for the failures we have endured. In doing so, we hand the responsibility for our happiness to them. Blame limits how we experience the fullness of who we are. Do we blame because we are trying to avoid making the difficult decisions regarding the direction of our life? Or do we blame because we need a villain for our emotional wounds?

Another need would be our need to criticize or judge others. This need originates from a desire to make ourselves feel better by putting others down. Our judgement can boost our self-image, even though this image is not an accurate assessment of who we are.

A need to judge or criticize also comes from a lack of self-love. We believe that by judging we will feel better about ourselves, although behaving this way will leave us feeling hollow and emotionally empty.

To fill the void, we make a habit of this behavior, thereby moving from one negative thought to another. The point to remember is there is no love in judgement, even if we think our judgement is justified.

It's possible we can become addicted to our needs. They

feed us a diet of thoughts, (although some are unhealthy), that give us a sense of purpose. If we continue this behavior, we distance ourselves from our authentic truth. Rather than live through the love found at the core of our being, we live a life devoid of any true meaning.

When we learn to shift our focus away from the negative needs we have come to believe as beneficial, we open the door to freely loving ourselves and others. With this elevated state of consciousness, supported by love, we no longer have the need to control the behavior of those around us.

Needs can be either harmful or supportive to our emotional health. Along the path to living a meaningful life, we will discover a need to share our love without conditions or expectations. This is the intention of living authentically, to fulfill our need to love without limitations.

Noise

THE WORLD CAN BE A VERY noisy place. Trucks, jets, barking dogs, and phones ringing, to name just a few. We can do little about most of the noise we hear in the outside world. It can sometimes be so noisy we don't even realize it until we step into a quiet place.

The same can be said for the noise within our own head. It can be a constant stream of chatter, thoughts that want to be addressed, needs that beg to be fulfilled, and ideas waiting for action. Not to mention the voices of our self-doubt, and negative self-talk.

The noise in our head may at times be more unbearable than the noise we experience from the outside world. Does it have to be this way? Can we silence the chatter allowing us to hear the voice of our authentic self?

Much of the gibberish playing through our head can easily be ignored, yet we give it a voice when we think it needs attention. Recently, in my morning meditation, I thought about a situation that happened many years ago. Why did I allow that thought to enter my mind at that moment in time? That memory had nothing to do with anything going on in my current reality.

Why did I allow a thought to disrupt my meditation, adding noise to an otherwise peaceful experience? To be honest, I lost focus, allowing the chatter to fill my head. I needed to strengthen my concentration, giving me the ability to silence this type of noise.

One way I practice muting the noise in my mind, is when unimportant thoughts arise, I tell them to go away. I then focus my attention elsewhere, to a more pleasing thought, or the stillness I'm trying to generate in my head.

When we silence the noise, we create a quiet space for our authentic self to be heard. Even though our higher self is speaking to us all the time, it doesn't shout, scream, or cry for attention as other sources of chatter.

We must turn down the volume of noise in our mind so we can begin to hear the messages our authentic self is sharing with us. At times we are so intent on silencing the chatter, we even silence the voice of our inner truth. This is because we may be unfamiliar with the sound of our authentic voice. We often confuse this loving voice with other sources of noise telling us we are less than we truly are.

Any message that tells us we are unworthy of living the best life possible is noise we should work to silence. The voice of our authentic self is always kind, loving, and supportive. This voice is constantly encouraging us to live to the fullness of who we are.

It may take time to learn to trust the voice of our authentic self because we have been fooled into thinking our self-doubt and negative self-talk are authentic. This will change as we learn that our authentic self has our best interest as its main focus.

As we journey through life guided by our authentic self, our noise level may increase. This is because our chatter still wants to be the main focus. In time our negative chatter will lose its ability to control us as we begin a life trusting our authentic self.

If the noise becomes too much to handle, concentrate on the message that is true and kind. This way we silence the noise by focusing on the loving voice of our authentic self.

Now

As much as we long for the past or hope for the future, all we have is this point in time. Nothing else matters but what we are experiencing in this moment. The here and now is where we will connect with our authentic self.

It can be difficult to remain focused in the present moment. There are many distractions and a great deal requiring our attention. In a sense, the busyness of life has found permanent residence in our consciousness, offering little space for stillness.

Yet, much of our life is created by the choices we make. If we are on the path to living a meaningful life, it's necessary to center ourselves in the here and now. This is where we begin to hear the quiet voice of our true self.

When we take a moment to silence the chatter floating around in our head, we allow ourselves the privilege of experiencing the world without limitations. These limitations may include our unfulfilled hopes and dreams, self-doubt, along with our preconceived ideas of how life should be unfolding. Without limitations, we see the world as it is, through the clarity of our connection with the Divine.

It's a common truth that now is all we have. There is no tomorrow, it's a dream, while yesterday is a memory. Yet we find ourselves moving between the future and the past with little regard for how we are living now. In behaving this way, we miss many opportunities to experience our authentic self.

We often assume there will be another time for sharing our love with others. In the digital world today, we have come to accept that emails, texts, and social media are more important than those sitting next to us right now. Is it because we think there will be time later for those we love?

History has shown how quickly life can change. In the blink of an eye, we could lose our ability to share or receive love. Is an email more important than being in the present moment? Does that text need immediate action, or can it wait until after our time with loved ones?

Now is all there is. By living an authentic life, we understand that there is no past, no future, only now. There is no time to waste on things that do not benefit our emotional well-being. We can yell at the evening news all we want, nothing will change. All it does is separate us from our ability to live in harmony with our true self.

By intentionally focusing on our "now moment" we will be the most connected with the truth of who we are. It is here where we can tap into an unlimited source of consciousness. This wisdom will guide us through life but can only be accessed in the present moment.

If we are too focused on the future or we are constantly reliving the past, we miss the guidance of our true self. To live an authentic life, we learn from our past, then move on. We understand we were not meant to remain in the past. We also recognize our future will be determined by our behavior in the here and now. The ability to live a meaningful life will be found in the wisdom of our now moment.

Meditation is one way to focus on the present. Although our

mind can be full of thoughts, we can observe these thoughts instead of becoming involved with them. Like watching clouds pass by, allow the thought to float away without attachment. When we master this in meditation, we can transfer this skill to our everyday life.

This takes practice because we have become accustomed to interacting with our thoughts whenever they arise. With time we can develop the emotional strength to silence the mental chatter generated by our thoughts. It is here we uncover the serenity of the present moment.

When we arrive at a place of stillness, we can live fully in the moment. Our focus becomes centered in the here and now, nothing matters but this place in time.

Experiencing the now moment provides us the opportunity to commit ourselves fully to the situation without compromise or distractions. When our attention is in the here and now, we give our loved ones the fullness of who we are. Now is where we have the opportunity to reconnect with our true self, although we must be strong enough to separate ourselves from the distractions preventing us from reaching this powerful place of truth.

Observe

How much do we see when we look? Do we notice the hawk soaring overhead? The ants carrying their heavy burdens? Or the sunlight filtering through the trees? What about the people we meet? Can we observe their behavior without judgement?

Is it possible to stop looking at things, and to teach ourselves to observe? When we observe there is nothing to find, no goals to accomplish. We are looking at the world without the need to judge, form an opinion, or even speak.

This requires us to quiet our mental chatter while we practice observing. When we arrive at a place of stillness, we begin to see and understand life on a deeper level. We will have silenced our inner dialogue that must always voice its opinion. Thereby allowing us to see life as it is, without the coloration of our preconceived ideas.

It can be difficult to observe our surroundings. Our mind is so busy focusing on other things, we may never experience the peacefulness of mental clarity. Oftentimes our eyes are searching for something that isn't there. We look for love in the wrong places, and we often seek comfort in uncomfortable situations. We ask for guidance from those who are looking for guidance from others. Because of this, we will never experience the peace of mind that is beneficial for our well-being.

We often view the world in a certain way. When it doesn't fit our vision, we compare it to how we would like it to be. Yet if we quiet our mind and observe, we begin to see a connection between our thoughts and how we perceive the world. In a way, observing gives us the opportunity to step away from our limited view of life, allowing us to see things on a bigger scale.

Quieting the mind while observing is like meditating. We see what is going on around us, but we choose not to become involved with it. In meditation, if a thought arises, we are taught to observe it without letting it disturb our peaceful state of mind.

The key to observing is not getting emotionally caught up in what we see. Can we observe the disagreeable behavior of others while maintaining our emotional center? Choosing to avoid falling into the trap of negativity by observing gives us the strength to remain silent, without judgement. The behavior of others reflects who they are, and our reaction to them tells the world who we are. When we observe without the need to respond, we connect with our authentic self.

Imagine watching the shadows of clouds move across the landscape or noticing a spider spinning a web. When we learn to observe, our inner stillness deepens. Along the way, our vision expands to see that which we cannot see when we are fixated on the negativity we may experience in life.

The intention of observing is to relax the mind, allowing us a few moments of silence, giving way to a sense of deep clarity. An interesting thing about quieting our mind is we will notice more moments of inspiration. How often have we arrived at a solution when we weren't thinking of the problem? At times being too focused can limit how we overcome challenges.

With the way the world works, we are taught to keep our head down, while pushing through our difficulties. Yet with this mindset, we may walk right past the solutions we are seeking. If we give ourselves the opportunity to observe, we may notice the answers in plain sight.

As with any new skill, observing takes practice. We are quick to judge, limiting the way we view the world. By learning to observe before we make a decision or move forward, we will have a better idea of which direction to travel.

Through the practice of observing, we will notice more when we look, hear more when we are silent, and say more when we speak. By being observant, we silence our mental chatter, giving us the ability to walk in unison with the truth of who we are.

One

You are the one, the one who can change your life. The one who can lead you through life's challenges. You are the only one who can discover the truth of who you are.

This cannot be left to others. No other person knows what is true and right for you, but you. The answers you seek are there waiting for you, yet you must be courageous enough to journey within. You are the one who holds the key to the door blocking your way forward. You are the one who has control of your life.

We often look to others for advice and inspiration, yet how often do we look in the mirror while asking for guidance? The face we see has answers, it's only a matter of learning to trust the voice within.

There can be much mental chatter preventing us from hearing our true inner voice. We must silence our negative self-talk, ignore our self-doubt; even disregard the advice of close friends to hear the voice of our own truth.

This may seem challenging because much of our life may have been built with the advice from our mental chatter. To be the person who supports ourselves along our spiritual journey we must refocus our attention on the one voice that speaks words of love and compassion.

You are the only person like you on Earth. No one like you has ever walked or will walk through life as you will. This makes you the one. You have a calling only you can manifest. But if we choose to seek guidance outside of ourselves, we may never reach our full potential.

To live to the fullness of who we are meant to be takes courage and determination. The world wants us to play it small so we don't cause any discomfort in the lives of those around us. Being the one may frighten the people who wish we would just step in line and fit in. Although if we succumb to who the world wants us to be, we will never see how far we can go.

Any great accomplishment, whether it is in art, literature, or science, has been achieved by someone who ignored their doubt as well as the doubt of those around them. They moved forward because they trusted themselves. They would rather fail moving forward, than regret sitting still trying to please others.

The powerful thing about choosing to be the one we turn to when times get tough, is that through our perseverance we will encourage others to be the one in their lives. Even if we think no one is watching, people see our courage and determination. Our behavior has the potential to ignite a fire within those who think an authentic life is out of reach. This will give them the strength needed to look within themselves with the intention of discovering their true self.

At the core of our being is a source of unconditional love. It is this love that drives us toward living an authentic life. When we connect with this love, we align with the truth of who we are. This is the key to opening the door to a life full of possibilities.

To live to the fullness of who we are takes courage. We must be the one who accepts responsibility for the choices we make and the outcome of these decisions. We set ourselves free when we take responsibility for the way our life is unfolding. We are the one who is responsible for the way our life turns out. By choosing to trust ourselves and the choices we make, we become the one who deserves an authentic life.

Oneness

W<small>HY IS IT A MOTHER KNOWS</small> when one of her children needs comfort, even if the child is a thousand miles away? Have you ever watched a flock of birds fly in unison, turning and diving as one being? Great herds of animals have been recorded moving across the vast landscape of Earth as one entity. Are these observations connected?

Humans tend to think that all there is in the world is us in our physical body, without any connection to other humans or the natural world around us. When we believe this way, we are thinking through our ego, which believes in individualism.

Could it be that all creatures, including humans, are connected by a stream of consciousness long forgotten by man? This can pose a challenge because this would mean that at one time humans were aware of this connection. What about those born into twins, knowing when the other sibling is in pain?

What if we were to accept that we are all connected to one stream of consciousness that at one time guided us through life? When we silence our ego and journey within to discover our authentic self, we come face to face with an eternal source of unconditional love. Could this love be the source of consciousness that connects us as one?

As we explore this love with more depth, we begin to realize that this love is the source of all life here and beyond our world. That would mean we are connected to all we can see, even deep into space. In this state of awareness, we realize the oneness of our existence, the belief that we are one with all creation.

Yet in the world today there is little consideration for those who appear different than us. Even a foreign language is seen as a barrier preventing us from recognizing our commonalities. But in truth we, as humans, have much more in common than we may be willing to believe. When we begin to live by the love at the center of all creation, we will notice how similar we are to each other, even if we do speak differently.

When we contemplate the idea of oneness, we must set aside our belief in individualism. Yes, we are all unique, with different passions and desires, although at our core we all hold within us the same flow of never-ending love.

Yet this love is often obscured by our need to explain that which we cannot explain. We talk about the flock of birds flying as one, they are just watching each other. A mother concerned about her distant child, it's just coincidence. Is this true?

To make humans comfortable we place things we cannot explain, or are too complicated to comprehend, into neat little compartments, with easy-to-understand labels. These labels bring us a sense of comfort, although they leave much unanswered. The idea of oneness may answer our questions because we have all come from the same source of creation.

Every element found in our body can be found in the soil. If each chemical is energy, then this energy vibrates at a certain frequency. When these elements are combined their total energy will also vibrate at a specific frequency.

All things on Earth maintain this powerful truth. This would mean that as a global population, humans are connected by the energy radiating from the elements found within our body.

Our individualism is only found on a surface level, everything else is a relationship to oneness, our connection to all that is. It is through our energetic link to each other that we begin to accept that we are one organism, in unison with all we can see in the night sky and beyond.

The idea of one consciousness can pose its challenges, because it forces us to look outside of our little compartments for answers. The clues may be in plain sight, if we are honest enough to challenge our beliefs and search for the common bond we have with each other, and the planet we inhabit.

Own It

Wнy is iт when things work out well for us, we accept all the credit, but when events fall apart, we run from our responsibility, pointing the finger of blame toward others? In a way, we will do whatever we can to avoid being the one who has to take responsibility for our own failures. What would happen if instead of behaving this way we owned our failures as well as our successes?

When we were children we never wanted to be accused of being at fault, so we would come up with excuses to avoid punishment — "The dog ate my homework." Yet as adults, we must take a different position and own our mistakes, and even our shortcomings.

This can be a challenge because we don't want to be seen as a failure, or a person who cannot be counted on. If we continue to sidestep accountability, we will never learn the important lessons failure has to teach us.

It's not only our actions we need to own. We must learn to own the words we speak. Being responsible for our words is the beginning of living an authentic life. No other person speaks through our mouth, so our words are our responsibility. We own them the moment they leave the tip of our tongue. Once said, our words are difficult to take back. The best way to keep our words in check is to listen to ourselves speak.

Owning our words and actions, begins with owning our thoughts as well. Everything we do and say starts with the thoughts we think. A slip of the tongue has a thought behind it, an unhealthy action has a thought supporting it.

By choosing to own our thoughts, words, and actions, we accept full responsibility for the outcome of our behavior. From this place of emotional maturity, we cannot accuse others of misunderstanding our intentions. We own what we have said and how we have acted. This is the path to living an authentic life.

If we take an honest look at our time on Earth, we will notice that no positive growth comes from avoiding our responsibility for something that didn't work out. Any lasting growth will be found in the lessons challenging situations teach us. When we are courageous enough to own our mistakes, we will benefit from these circumstances.

One of the difficulties with owning our behavior is we have to be truthful with ourselves. Sure, at times owning our actions may be painful, but this pain shows us that we recognize our errors and are willing to change and grow from the experience.

We could arrive at a point when we accept that owning our behavior, good or bad, is the quickest way to heal from a painful situation. If we constantly blame others, we are delaying any opportunity to heal from the pain. By avoiding our self-responsibility, we allow the wound to fester, until it becomes too painful to avoid. Here we have two basic choices, own our part in the experience, or turn away and let the pain continue to build.

Owning our behavior will have its challenges, but this is one way to know how we affect the world around us. As we begin the journey of becoming our authentic self, living a true life, we must own our thoughts, words, and actions. This way those around us can count on us to be honest and sincere.

P

Patience

Have you ever watched a cat sit by a gopher hole patiently waiting for the gopher to stick its head up to see if the coast is clear? The cat is in no rush, it seems it can sit there for hours; all it has to do is be patient.

Are we like the cat? Patient with the way our life is unfolding? Or are we racing to an imaginary finish line no one can see? Do we stop to notice how nature is patient? In spring the leaves burst out when the time is right. Everything in the natural world happens in its own time frame.

Humans can be the most impatient creatures on the planet. We wake up, rush to work, hurry home, fall into bed, then do it all over again the next day. We rush toward the weekend, only to speed off to work when it's over.

We want everything now without the patience to wait for it. Our focus can be so short-sighted we cannot see the long view, nor do we have the patience to take the necessary steps to discover the truth of who we are.

It takes work, courage, dedication, and patience to live to the fullness of who we are meant to be. We often live as if we are racing an invisible clock. In a way we are because our time on Earth is finite. But as we race through our day are we living a fulfilling life?

Imagine a book titled, *The Shortcut to Living a Meaningful Life*. This is how most of us want to live. Give us the shortcut, we have an appointment or an email to answer. We don't have the patience to meditate or listen to our higher self for guidance. Let's get this done, the shortcut version will do.

How meaningful would our lives be if we lived this way? To accomplish anything of value takes time. We cannot rush the rose to bloom, it will open when it's ready. Our impatience creates a false sense of importance, and discontent in our life. We are rushing, but we don't know why, or where we are going.

What if the meaning of life was to uncover the love at the core of our being, then to share this love with the world around us? We cannot hurry through this process, it takes patience.

We must allow ourselves the time needed to sift through our beliefs to see which ones benefit us, and those that limit the way we experience life. The beliefs that hinder our growth are those we should shed from our awareness.

This takes patience because we have built a life based on our beliefs. It will take time to shift our way of thinking. If we try to rush this, we will end up living a life that is not in alignment with our inner truth. We may rush the process because we don't want to take a deep look at the beliefs preventing us from realizing our authentic self.

Of course, we want to be there now, even if "there" is not a life that has any true meaning or value. We want to have it now, know it now, be the best now. We often do not want to do the hard work to discover our truth because it's difficult and we are impatient.

When we realize that creating an authentic life takes time, we become more patient. As we see the beneficial lessons life is teaching us, we will begin to understand that everything happening to us has a reason. If we are patient, we will learn why things unfold as they do. This way we can use the flow of life to our advantage, taking time to become the best version of ourselves.

We do not have to rush through life. We can stop to smell the roses, volunteer in our community, or pursue a passion. The intention of life is to reconnect with the truth of who we are. Having patience will allow us to enjoy the journey.

Persistence

A CHINESE PROVERB SAYS, "THE JOURNEY of a thousand miles begins with a single step." The challenge becomes one of taking the first step then continuing to move forward with each new step. But we always have choices. Do we begin the journey in the first place when the destination seems so far away? Or do we place one foot in front of the other, moving toward an understanding of ourselves we would never receive anywhere else? The outcome of our life will be determined by the choices we make.

Nothing in life happens without some sort of action. If we want to create an authentic life, we must sift through our thoughts and beliefs, shedding those not serving our best interest. Think of negative thoughts or beliefs as an anchor holding us in place, preventing us from experiencing the fullness of who we are.

Living an authentic life takes persistence. It's easy to fall back into old, unhealthy patterns of behavior. There will be temptations and distractions taking our focus away from our goals. When this happens we lose momentum, our discipline falters, we then struggle to regain our footing.

If our goals align with the truth of who we are, we will find the courage to keep moving forward. There is a Japanese proverb that says, "Fall down seven times, get up eight times." Life can be difficult, with many unforeseen challenges, yet to live an honest life we must carry on despite these challenges.

Persistence is a combination of inner motivation, fueled by self-discipline. It can be easy to complain about how life does not equal our expectations, but it is important to remember, we are the creators of our reality. When we decide to see how far we can go, we will have to accomplish this one step at a time.

One of the struggles we may face along the road of life is realizing we are the ones who have to do the inner work. No other person can do this for us. We must look in the mirror of our consciousness and accept responsibility for how our life is progressing.

This may not be easy because at times we would rather sit on the front porch and watch the world go by. It takes persistence to get up each and every day with the intention of pursuing our dreams and goals.

A time may come when we will be our only cheerleader. Others may not see our dreams as well as we do. Nor can we ask them to support us if they disagree with the direction of our journey. We must find the inner strength to keep moving forward no matter what obstacles we come upon, or what other people think.

Our comfort zone is always calling us back to its warmth and familiarity. Like an old friend who knows our weaknesses, our comfort zone enjoys our company. At some level, we know this old friend does not have our best interest as its main priority. We must separate ourselves from its grasp and continue moving forward. Our desire to succeed, our persistence, will help us overcome the hold comfort has on us.

If we want to create a better life, we must work at it. No one will give us the life we want to live. We must do something to accomplish our dreams. We must learn to trust ourselves and silence the mental chatter to hear the voice of our intuition leading us through life's challenges.

At times we will want to give up, throw in the towel, call it quits. Although understandable, how will we feel when we realize we were so close to succeeding? This is not who we are, we want to live a life aligned with the truth at the core of our being. Following this dream, this goal, takes persistence, we do what we can to keep moving forward.

We may not see the path ahead clearly, yet we will have a feeling, a knowing, if our journey is true and right, so we continue. The only way to know how far we can go is to begin with a single step. To live an authentic life may not be easy, but we will learn more about ourselves than had we chosen to remain in our comfort zone.

Practice

IN LIFE, IT SEEMS WE ARE given the test first, then we are taught the lesson. It may appear backward, but this could be the best approach to gaining wisdom and understanding. That way we can practice what the lesson has taught us until the next test.

What if we shifted our point of view and considered life a practice? How often do we get anything right on the first try? By looking at life as a practice, we take away the power of self-judgement, thereby accepting that we are always improving.

No matter how challenging our life may become, we can benefit from the lessons life teaches. This is only possible if we shift our attention toward what we need to learn from the experience. We can use these lessons to better ourselves through our ability to practice what life has taught us.

Every once in a while we stumble, losing our focus, causing us to fall back into unhealthy emotional patterns. If we are courageous enough we can use these situations as opportunities for positive growth. But this awareness takes practice because when we fall off the wagon, we may become our own worst enemy.

When this happens our negative self-talk may be the only voice we hear within us. This discouraging chatter has no love or kindness for us. So, it may take a while before we return to our emotional center.

We often criticize ourselves for losing focus. Yet why is that? Is it because we think we are failures if we don't get it right the first time? It takes practice to become good at anything. Why is life any different?

If we want to live an authentic life, we must change the way we think about our difficulties. Is it possible to see them as opportunities to practice living through these challenges with ease and grace?

Practicing as we go through life seems like a crazy idea. But think about it. With each new experience we can work on being our best self every time. This may be difficult at first. Although with increased awareness and practice, we will know how to handle these situations when they arise again in the future.

Reframing life as a practice may take some of the self-inflicted pressure off ourselves. So often we have been taught to get it right the first time. If we don't, we are considered failures. There is no positive growth from this mindset. Yet if we choose to accept life as a practice, we give ourselves the benefit of the doubt.

In this positive state of mind, we can accept that we are doing our best, given what we know at the time. It is here where we release our need for harsh self-judgement often associated with our perceived failures.

Focusing on life as a practice gives us a better chance to live to the fullness of who we are. A job that doesn't work out becomes a learning experience rather than a failed attempt at success. The same would be true for our relationships. There is always something beneficial to learn from the things that don't work out like we had planned.

Failure should not stop us from moving forward toward

realizing the truth of who we are. Being true to ourselves may never be easy. But if we choose to look at life as a practice, any obstacle or test we face will now be seen as a steppingstone on the path to living an authentic life.

Prayer

When we contemplate the word prayer, we often think of kneeling in prayer before going to sleep. Or, being in a place of worship, seeking comfort and guidance. But what if we were to consider our everyday actions as a form of prayer?

Would we then behave in a way that shows our appreciation for all we have, and the abundance around us? Is it possible we would be more compassionate and understanding if we regarded our behavior as a prayer?

If we were to treat our actions as a form of devotion, intended to benefit the global population, we may become more aware of how we go through our day. Even if we do not believe in a source of consciousness that connects all of us together, we must realize that our actions radiate energy out to the world, affecting everyone.

Imagine our every thought, word, and action, as a prayer. In a way this prayer becomes the way we walk through life. If we are positive, loving, and kind, then our actions will radiate this positive energy, influencing those we encounter. As we go through life this way, our behavior becomes a prayer of gratitude and compassion.

You could ask, "Why is prayer important?" Think of our conduct as an advertisement broadcasting to the world who we are. Every word we speak is heard loud and clear. Each action we take is seen by everyone. Would our behavior be a prayer of kindness and love? Or would it be a list of blame and complaints, a "who's who" of who hurt us, a dialogue of negativity about the things that have happened in our life? This would be the absence of prayer.

There is much written about the healing power of true, authentic prayer. When we live a loving, compassionate life, we are living a life of prayer. In doing so, with each positive word we are healing ourselves and those we are with. With every action founded on kindness we will be elevating the consciousness of all people.

The root of all prayer is the love found within our heart. For a prayer to be meaningful, it must have a foundation of love, otherwise it is just a worthless group of words. If loving prayer is the path to healing, then wouldn't it be best to act in a way that accesses this love?

Knowing our behavior is a prayer for well-being and healing, allows us to focus on what is best for us and the world around us. This gives us the opportunity to heal emotionally as we go about our day. We may be too busy to take the time to kneel in prayer, but if our actions are positive, then everything we do will become a prayer, benefiting our physical and emotional health.

Is it too much to contemplate our behavior as a prayer? It could be, but rather than focusing on the negatives we see in the world, we can have a positive effect by accepting that when we behave with love, kindness, and compassion we are indeed praying for our well-being, and that of the global population.

Quality

How would we define a quality life? Is it living to the fullness of who we are? Have we chosen to remain small, avoiding the work needed to live a quality life? Do we settle for less because we are too afraid of what the future may hold? Are we surrounding ourselves with people who help bring out our best qualities?

The quality of our life will be determined by many variables. No matter what choices we make, our thoughts and beliefs will have the biggest impact on the way we walk through life. In the early 1960s, George Fuechsel, an IBM programmer and instructor, was credited with coining the term, "Garbage in, garbage out." Although this might have to do with inputting information into a computer, it can also be attributed to our thoughts, beliefs, and the outcome of our choices.

If we believe we create our life experience through the thoughts we think, it would be to our advantage to have quality thoughts. Seems easy, doesn't it? Though it can be more difficult than we think.

Every experience we have, positive or negative, will influence our thoughts, thereby impacting the quality of our life. It makes no difference if we are holding a cute puppy, hear a negative story on the news, or read a derogatory comment on a social media post. These events dictate the course of our thoughts, affecting the way we view the world.

The key to living a quality life is to pay attention to our thoughts and the outcome of our actions. If our intention is to live a life of true meaning, we must be aware of how our thoughts affect the quality of our life. Quality thoughts produce quality actions, it can be no other way.

The quality of our thoughts also holds true when we think about ourselves. If we believe our negative self-talk and self-doubt, we will create a self-image based on these thoughts. Living an authentic life gives us the strength to dismiss these streams of negative thinking, allowing us the freedom to fill our mind with positive, self-loving thoughts and beliefs.

It is not only our thoughts in need of our attention. For a quality life, being aware of the people we consider friends is critical. Are they people who validate our negative way of thinking and behaving, thereby limiting our possibilities? Or are they supportive as we journey to discover our inner truth? Do we notice their absence when we cross a milestone?

We may believe the influence of those around us will not affect the quality of our life, but we would be wrong. Having friends who bolster our negative behavior will keep us repeating the same harmful patterns. Is it possible we fail to realize that the quality of people we associate with will determine the trajectory of our life?

A quality life is earned, it is not something that just happens. If we want to live to our fullness, it is essential to do the work to clear away old, unhealthy needs and patterns of behavior. This requires constant attention to how we interact with the world around us.

We often try to fool ourselves into thinking we are living authentically. Yet if we take time for self-reflection, we may notice we are experiencing the same story over and over again.

Has blame become our "go to" emotion? How often do we take responsibility for the way life unfolds? As we move closer to our inner truth, it is important to become aware of how our behavior creates our life experiences.

There may be little we can do when life becomes difficult, except choose the best mindset possible. Our reaction toward these difficulties will determine if the outcome is favorable or not. Learning to control our thoughts and behavior when challenges arise, will give us the ability to work through these situations as best we can.

Looking toward the future, we realize the quality of our life will depend on how emotionally centered we are in the present moment. Whatever happens to us has the potential to launch us forward or hold us back. The quality of our thoughts and actions will dictate which path we choose.

Quiet

OUR WORLD IS A BUSY PLACE with many distractions. Oftentimes our focus wavers because of the external stimulation we experience throughout the day. It seems our attention span has diminished because there is much in life that demands our participation. At times we feel exhausted, but we are unsure why.

As we journey toward uncovering our authentic self, we realize that guidance flows to us in many ways. The challenge becomes one of finding a quiet place to hear and acknowledge this wisdom.

Yet, setting aside time for quiet is not only limited to silencing the noise of the outside world. Creating quiet within ourselves gives us the opportunity to recognize the guidance originating from our higher self.

The difficulty begins in determining which guidance is worth following and which we should ignore. People often believe that loud is strong and quiet is weak. This is not the case when considering the wisdom of our true self. Even though this guidance is constantly being sent to us, we may not have the ability to hear this wisdom because of the noise within our mind as well as that of the outside world.

If we seek to unite with our authentic self, it is essential to learn to quiet the chatter within. The voices of our negative self-talk, self-doubt, and false beliefs, seem to constantly flood our mind with nonsense. Yet we often choose to focus on these voices because they are the loudest.

The wisdom of our true self speaks to us in many forms. This guidance could be a gut feeling, a gentle voice, or a tingling sensation, to name a few. It can be difficult to separate this guidance from the chatter we often hear in our mind.

One way to discern if the guidance is from our higher self is to ask if the foundation of this wisdom is rooted in love. If we listen to the noise bombarding us each and every day, we notice that much of this is without love. Yet for some reason we believe this racket is true because it's the loudest. Cultivating our ability to find quiet within ourselves takes practice. It can be too easy focusing on the negativity of our self-doubt.

Think of quiet as a reconnection with our inner truth. Imagine a secure place where we meet with our authentic self. Here we can speak honestly, revealing our deepest fears, while feeling safe and loved. We know we are protected because there is nothing but love for us in this quiet setting.

With practice we can develop the ability to return to our quiet place when difficulties arise. As we become more comfortable silencing our negative mental chatter, the love of our higher self will comfort us whenever life is challenging.

In this new awareness we learn to find quiet in the outside world as well. When the noise of life becomes too much, we can return to our place of quiet. This will give us the chance to take a step back, to notice what is important and what is not worth our time. The intention is to create a few moments of quiet in the middle of a hectic world. Thereby allowing us the ability to return to our emotional center.

In this quiet place we can hear the guidance from our authentic self clearly. We know this wisdom is true because of the love we will feel. As we learn to trust this guidance, our self-confidence will strengthen and we will reinforce our ability to see beyond our limiting beliefs. Our desire to speak our truth will be life changing.

When we learn to quiet the noise surrounding us, we open the door to living an authentic life. It is here in this sanctuary of quiet, we uncover the truth of who we are.

Quit

For many people, the word "Quit" is not part of their vocabulary. They believe they should push through any challenge that may arise. Some feel that if they quit, they will be seen as losers, or unreliable…not labels we want associated with who we show to the world.

What if we were to reshape our beliefs about quitting? Why is it difficult to quit a job that makes us unhappy? Leave a relationship that is not loving or kind? Or walk away from people who do not see our true worth? Quitting unhealthy situations can open the door to better circumstances.

If we are passionate about our dreams, but are struggling to move forward, then quitting may not be the best option. Each struggle has its own set of lessons that will benefit us in the long term. We may never know how close we are to fulfilling our dreams. If we choose to quit, we will never find out.

I once had a job that didn't align with my truth. It was challenging to be at work because I felt out of place. When I tried to look into the future, I realized I would always stay in that position because there was no room for advancement. I wasn't happy, nor did I feel satisfied. So I quit.

Our life and happiness are our responsibility, not that of our partner, our parents, or our employer. Yet we often remain in unhealthy situations because we are afraid to quit and seek better options.

When the opinions of others matter more to us than our own opinion of ourselves then their opinions control us. To live an authentic life, we must learn to focus on what is true and right for us, no matter what others think or say.

This can be challenging because we often seek the approval of others to boost our self-esteem. We don't want to quit because their opinion of us matters to our worth. Thinking of it this way, we are living a life where it is more important to please others, than it is to please ourselves.

Many bestselling books have been rejected by numerous publishers. Yet the authors, who believed in the value of their work, chose not to quit and continued querying agents and publishers. Their belief in their work prevented them from quitting. Many of these same authors quit their jobs and left situations that were unfulfilling or made them feel worthless.

There is a time and place where quitting is advantageous and when it is not. After quitting my unfulfilling job, I found a situation that fit my needs. I felt my skills were appreciated and there was room for advancement. In this case quitting was beneficial to my emotional health.

We all have weak moments in life when we feel the world is against us. Yet deep within us is a loving voice cheering us on to greatness. When we silence the voice of our self-doubt and ignore our negative self-talk, we will begin to hear this caring voice.

This voice may be telling us to quit an unhealthy situation, or it may be telling us to focus on only the next step, then the next step after that. This is the voice of our authentic self, guiding us through the challenges of life.

If we choose to quit, we may find a better situation if we listen to the guidance spoken by our authentic self. If we choose to stay, we may realize how close we are to living a passionate life. The choice is always ours.

Question

ALONG THE PATH TO REALIZING OUR authentic self, we find it necessary to question everything we have been taught. The intention is to determine if we are living in alignment with the truth of who we are. For some, this might stop the journey in its tracks, although this will be where we experience our true self.

Throughout life, we create a persona to please those around us. The role we play contains parts of who we are but does not reflect the entirety of our being. The reason is people expect a certain identity from us, even if this is not who we are now.

At some point it's essential to question why we behave as we do. Is it because we are seeking acceptance from others? Are we too afraid to reveal our true self to the world, thinking our persona will protect us from hardship? Don't we understand that by being someone we are not, we are separating ourselves from our authentic truth?

As we maintain this way of life, our persona becomes a walled enclosure keeping our authentic self from view, while denying ourselves the ability to live truthfully. We may go through our entire life living this way. Or we may recognize the root cause of our unhappiness and begin the healing process by questioning why.

Think of questioning ourselves as breaking down the walls we once thought protected us. As scary as it might be to expose our true self to others, it is not as unsettling as living a life disconnected from the truth of who we are.

Questioning ourselves may be frightening, but this course of action will set us free. Free to live by the truth found at the core of our being. It's not hard to come up with a question. It's arriving at an honest answer that can be difficult. Being honest is crucial to freeing ourselves from the beliefs limiting our ability to live fully.

We must question our thoughts, beliefs, and actions, to see if they align with our inner truth. If they are negative, ask why we hold them in our consciousness. The foundation of our beliefs and actions is our thoughts. That's why questioning a thought can shift our behavior.

When I began questioning my thoughts, I noticed how many thoughts were based on information I had received from others. I had no first-hand knowledge on the subject, but for some reason I held onto these second-hand thoughts. Once I realized the thought was useless, I was able to release it from my awareness, never to be thought of again.

It is important to remember, our thoughts create our beliefs and actions. To question a thought means we also question our behavior. I have come to the realization that any thought not founded on love is worth discarding from my consciousness. This way I do the best I can to maintain beliefs and actions rooted in love.

The challenge begins when we move away from the persona we have created to please others. Their expectation of who they want to see may not align with our rediscovered truth. We may lose friends or disconnect from family members. The attraction to remain as we were, is strong.

People are comfortable with who we were, not with who we

are now. Yet we cannot allow their expectations to determine the direction of our lives. It is up to them to question why they want us to remain as we were.

Once we are comfortable with questioning ourselves, it will become second nature. If a negative thought arises, we automatically question why. If we fall back into old patterns of behavior, again we question why. The answers will benefit our journey.

The intention of questioning what we have been taught throughout life is to uncover the truth of who we are meant to be. Questioning ourselves is a powerful act of self-love, yet it takes courage to see it this way. We may be too afraid to begin this life changing work, yet if we want to live to the fullness of who we are, we must become comfortable questioning ourselves.

R

Regret

On the last day of life, will we be filled with regret? Will we regret we hadn't gone after our dreams, or said "I love you" one more time? Will we regret we hadn't been more understanding, supportive, or positive? Will we regret not forgiving ourselves, or those who knew nothing different?

Much to contemplate, yet if you are reading this, it means you have time to clear away any regrets you may be holding within your consciousness. You have the ability to resolve your regrets if you are strong enough to forgive yourself and accept that you did the best you could.

Regrets are anchors preventing us from living to the fullness of who we are. They sabotage our relationships and limit the way we experience the world. Yet when we choose to live regret free, life begins anew.

There are many kinds of regrets. I regret not running the 1,500-meter when in high school. I always wonder how quickly I could have run that iconic event. This kind of regret is different than the regret of not telling someone how much I loved them one more time before they passed away.

I can do nothing about either case, although I can accept I did the best I could. Then forgive myself, thereby allowing my regret to teach me the importance of being in the present moment. There's a chance I could be so deep in my regret I might miss the possibilities that pass by me each day.

The thing about regret is it's a judgement of our past. We judge ourselves for not doing enough, being enough, or not living to the best of our ability. When we look over our past, we may see many reasons to regret.

Although there is an opposite side to regret we fail to notice. We can appreciate all the positive things we accomplished, the life we did live, the words we did say, and the lives we influenced by these inspiring words and actions.

If we take an honest look at our lives, we may recognize more reasons to be pleased with ourselves than we have reasons to be regretful. Yet it is our regrets that continue to keep us feeling we aren't good enough.

I may regret not running the 1,500 meters, but I can refocus and be proud of the times I placed in the top three in the 800 meters. It is all a matter of where we choose to place our focus.

Regrets can also inspire us to do great things. We may regret a missed opportunity, but if something similar comes our way, we may take the chance and use it to the best of our ability. In this way we are using our regrets to improve ourselves so we can live a better life.

There may be events in life that are no longer possible for us to accomplish. If we regret these things, we might miss an opportunity to do something completely different, yet much more beneficial. Our regrets cloud our vision of what is possible.

Yes, I regret not telling those whom I love how much they meant to me before they transitioned, I have learned from this regret. I also regret saying words I cannot take back, a powerful lesson in being aware of my words.

Regrets can control us or can expand our awareness of what

is possible. It will all depend on where we place our focus, and what we do with the wisdom we have learned.

As with many negative emotions, regret has a root cause. Do we regret because we are angry we have unfulfilled dreams? If so, what is currently preventing us from pursuing these dreams? We can easily disarm our regret by taking the necessary steps needed to accomplish our goals.

Small steps taken with honesty and authenticity will give us the ability to move forward without regret. We always regret it when we do nothing, yet we are filled with positive energy when we take the steps needed to succeed.

With each new day we have the opportunity to choose to remain in our regrets or take the challenge and move past them. We can learn much from our regrets allowing them to fade from view, as an authentic, fulfilling life comes into focus.

Resilience

How quickly do we bounce back after falling flat on our face or losing the concentration to remain focused? Have we accepted the limiting beliefs of others as fact, hindering our ability to become successful? Can we access the self-discipline needed to ignore our self-doubt and silence our negative self-talk, thereby giving us the emotional strength to be resilient when we fail?

Throughout much of life we will face many obstacles. These roadblocks have the power to knock us down, keeping us there if we choose to accept defeat.

To live to the fullness of who we are requires resilience. We must get up after every failure, setback, or distraction. At first this might seem difficult, but the lessons we need to learn to live authentically will be found in the challenges we face.

We often think only strong-minded people are resilient. What we fail to understand is resilience is like weightlifting. The more weights we lift, the stronger we become. The same can be said of resilience, the more challenges we overcome, the more resilient we will be in the future.

An interesting aspect of life is we are given the test before we are handed the information we need to pass the test. This means we often get knocked down before we have what we need to prevent the failure. But after the experience we definitely have what we need to move forward. Isn't that the definition of resilience? Getting back up after a failure?

Life can become frustrating when we face roadblock after roadblock. This is one reason we lose enthusiasm and give up. The thing about giving up is we may never know how close we were to accomplishing our goal. If we walk away now, we may regret it for the remainder of our life.

Being resilient takes stamina and focus. It can be too easy to believe our self-doubt and negative self-talk. These two sources of negativity can stop us in our tracks. Yet if we realize these negative voices have been taught to us throughout life, we begin to ignore their useless chatter.

Much of what we believe about ourselves has been learned from those around us. If they doubt us, they tell us repeatedly. When we fail it is those close to us who may remind us of our failures. These are people who claim to love and support us, yet their words do not align with their love for us.

It can be discouraging to be surrounded by people who do not see our dreams as clearly as we do. When others doubt us, we must find the strength to ignore their advice. Only we know what is true and right for us. It is this knowing that will maintain our resilience when difficulties arise.

Our ability to bounce back from unexpected setbacks begins with the love we have for ourselves. The strength of our self-love gives us the courage to see the positive lessons in all our misfortunes and misunderstandings.

When we are aware of our self-love, the negative comments of others no longer affect the way we walk through life. We love ourselves enough to disregard what others say or think about us and our journey.

Using the strength of our self-love, we know what is true and right for us without the need for validation from those around us. Even if we fall flat on our face, our self-love gives us the resilience to get up, brush off the dirt, then continue moving forward.

Oftentimes we judge ourselves on our successes, but the true measure of our character will be determined by our resilience after a failure. There is much in life we cannot control. Although we <u>can</u> control how we behave when a roadblock appears on our journey.

The way we handle these unforeseen challenges will give us an opportunity to understand the truth of who we are. How we decide to overcome these challenges will reveal to us our inner strength. The success we have to overcome any challenge will be found in our ability to think outside the scope of our limitations.

If we choose defeat, we have accepted a way of life that will never lead us to our full potential. Our resilience when challenges and failures arise will help us break down the barriers preventing us from living an authentic life. It is in this place of strength and self-love we begin to recognize the truth of who we are.

Resistance

It is said, "That which we resist, persists." It's an interesting thought because we assume what we resist will go away or move on. Yet if we look at it from a different angle, we recognize its truth.

We often do our best to push away the things we don't want. But for some reason they keep appearing. Is it possible to examine our past to see how often we tried to resist events or people to no avail? Think of resistance as the more we push against something, the more that "something" will be a part of our life.

Our resistance is a form of magnet. With more resistance we attract back similar energy. This is where we notice that what we don't want keeps showing up in life. We think if we keep pushing things away, they will leave, but we soon notice that is not often the case.

Resistance is much like riding a bicycle with the brake on. We may be moving forward, but our resistance prevents us from progressing through life with ease. The only way to make the bicycle go faster is to release the brake.

Life is similar. If we intend to live a fulfilling life we must release our need to resist change. It is scary to seek new ways of thinking and living. At first, be comfortable with being uncomfortable. New ways of thought will challenge our beliefs, possibly shaking our fragile foundation.

Our fear of moving toward an authentic life prevents us from living truthfully. Think of negativity as resistance. Any negative thought, belief, or action is a form of resistance. Once we notice when we are behaving in a negative fashion, we will recognize how often we are resisting a meaningful life.

Resistance could also be considered a form of control. Along our journey to living a meaningful life, there will be much we cannot control. The fear of letting go of our need to control the uncontrollable will keep us from living the best life possible. We must let go, then step into the unknown before we can live to the fullness of who we are.

We could say the opposite of resistance is to go with the flow. But this can also frighten us because we may have no idea in which direction to travel. It is easier to remain in our comfort zone than it is to strike off on the journey of self-discovery.

It might be easy to identify the source of our resistance. Oftentimes resistance can be found in the voices of our self-doubt and negative self-talk. Yet we will also find resistance in many of the thoughts and beliefs we have been taught throughout life.

If we take a closer look at the chatter floating around in our head, we will notice much of this noise is negative, and most of it is not supportive. This means our own thoughts and beliefs are limiting the way we move through life. In other words, our resistance to living a meaningful experience is self-inflicted.

Yes, of course we will face challenges outside of our control, yet we have the ability to overcome these difficulties once we commit to living an authentic life. Our dedication to live authentically releases us from the fear of the unknown. The way forward may still be unknown, yet we now have the courage to move ahead.

The intention is to live a life that surpasses our wildest dreams. We cannot go halfway. A halfhearted attempt at life is riding our bike, holding onto the brake, wondering why we are not getting where we want to go.

When we choose to let go of our resistance, we are flooded with wisdom and guidance unlike anything we have experienced. Our commitment to living our best life opens the door to the people and situations that will help us accomplish anything true to our heart. To live to the fullness of who we are, it is best to release our resistance, thereby allowing life to flow.

Revenge

I OFTEN WONDER WHY WE BELIEVE revenge is a viable option. Could it be we think our revenge will even the score? Why are we keeping score in the first place? Is revenge the great equalizer we believe it to be?

Oftentimes when we are hurt by others, our first reaction is to seek revenge. We imagine different scenarios where we have the upper hand, thereby giving us the ability to inflict punishment.

In our version of revenge we cause pain to those who caused our suffering. But do we ever consider revenge as another form of suffering? Does our revenge move us forward toward healing and a loving state of mind? Or is our revenge keeping us connected to the people who caused our pain?

The best question to ask ourselves before we walk the dark path of vengeance would be, "Is our revenge beneficial to our emotional growth?" Sure, acts of revenge might feel good for a short time, yet will this behavior set us free?

One thing often overlooked when we have been hurt by others, is our need to heal as quickly as possible. Can we learn what is necessary to better prepare ourselves if a similar encounter arises in the future? Don't we realize that when we heal, we grow stronger emotionally?

Walking away from a painful situation with the intention of learning from the experience is the best we can do for our emotional health. If we choose to act in a vengeful manner, we are making the choice to keep the negative energy active in our consciousness.

Little do we know, our desire to seek revenge begins to control us emotionally. Rather than letting go and moving on, the negativity surrounding revenge keeps us emotionally stagnate.

Although not healthy, for some reason we enjoy seeing others in pain because of what they have done to us. As we examine our need for revenge, we notice there is a lack of love for ourselves and others in our behavior.

When we choose to retaliate, we are doing so from the lower levels of consciousness. We decide revenge is the option that will make us feel powerful. Yet this power is filled with shame, and little to no self-love. We cannot claim to love ourselves while beginning a course of vengeful actions.

We often forget our healing is our responsibility. No matter what others have done to us, our ability to heal begins with our willingness to let go and move on. Holding tightly to our pain while seeking revenge will lead us deeper and deeper into the abyss of self-loathing. We cannot begin to heal or love ourselves if we choose revenge.

No matter how much revenge takes place, we will never feel complete or whole behaving this way. A part of us will still be feeding our desire for revenge, believing it is justified. The more we seek revenge, the more we add to our shame. Being vengeful is not a place of power. It is a state of weakness. We may think being vengeful gives us strength, but it does not.

If we have been harmed by others, the best we can do for ourselves is to search for ways to begin the healing process. Their actions reflect who they are, while our ability to heal is confirmation of the love we have for ourselves.

To live to the fullness of who we are, it is important to step away from the negativity of a revenge mindset. Our way forward will be found in self-forgiveness. We forgive ourselves for falling into the trap of believing revenge is the answer.

We have no control over how others act, yet we have complete control of how we behave. Even if we hurt someone and they choose the road of revenge, we do not have to become involved in their actions.

Our behavior may have harmed others. In this case, we can apologize. We can also forgive them for seeking the negative path of revenge. Yet we can also forgive ourselves for our transgressions.

The way forward from any painful experience is to learn what we can, then vow to do better in the future. A state of mind that seeks revenge will not allow us to walk toward a healthier way of life.

We will always be chained to the negativity of lower levels of consciousness if revenge is our option. If the intention is to live to the fullness of who we are, we must set aside our need to make others pay for their negative behavior. This way we are free from the restraints we place on ourselves when we choose revenge.

S

Sacrifice

THERE IS MUCH WRITTEN ON THE virtue of sacrifice. We are taught that to live a spiritual life, we must sacrifice ourselves in some way. Yet what would happen if we were to discover the truth of who we are, then dedicate our life to living by this truth? We wouldn't have to sacrifice any aspect of our being to justify our spiritual journey.

When we discover our authentic self, we connect with an eternal source of unconditional love. Our lives will then be guided by this powerful stream of love. In living this way, we would be the embodiment of love. Our every thought, word, and action would have a foundation rooted in love. It would be this love that will guide us throughout our day.

The idea of sacrificing for the good of others teaches us to ignore the desires that will benefit us in any way. Over time our sacrifice may plant the seeds of bitterness or resentment. In a way, the actions we take with the intention of reaching deeper levels of spirituality may cause us to become angry or discouraged.

Imagine how those we intend to help would feel when they become aware of our bitterness? Our actions will not be felt as authentic, because of the expectations we have of reaching spirituality by our sacrifice.

To give freely without anger or resentment, our behavior must be founded on unconditional love. It is here where our every thought, word, and action are created by the love found within us.

When love becomes the foundation of our actions, there will be no need to sacrifice, because we act out of love. Everything we think, do, or say is wrapped in love. We are not bitter because our actions align with our truth; a truth founded on love.

Rather than sacrifice ourselves because we believe this is the way to higher levels of spirituality, we realize the path to spirituality is through sharing our love without conditions or expectations. We help others because we love helping others, not because we believe there will be a reward for our service. Our actions are the reward in themselves.

If we are true to ourselves, and in alignment with the love at the core of our being, our love will be the foundation of our behavior. We will not need to sacrifice any aspect of who we are, because who we are is love. If we love supporting our children, there is no sacrifice. When we encourage our partner, there is no sacrifice, only love for our partner.

To arrive at this place of love, we must silence our mental chatter telling us to throw ourselves under the bus for those we claim to love. We can love freely without the need to sacrifice ourselves.

It may take time to readjust to this way of thinking, but in doing so, we will experience more love in our life, and in our heart. Sacrifice may be virtuous. Yet if it comes at the cost of not being true and authentic, we may want to discover the love at the center of who we are, then learn to share this love without the need to sacrifice our truth.

Service

Would we regard our actions as a service for the greater good? Or do we behave in a manner that only benefits ourselves? What if we were to see our actions as a way to lift global consciousness, thereby improving living conditions around the world?

Is it possible to consider our day-to-day actions an act of service benefiting others? A true service begins with the love found deep within our being. Why love? If our service is a way to boost our self-esteem because we lack awareness of our self-love, then our service is conditional.

If we accept that to love honestly and freely, is to love without condition or expectation, then a true act of service must be honest and free of expectations. Honest, because our service cannot be a façade for personal gain. Free, because we cannot expect a reward for our service if it is true and authentic.

It doesn't take much to see people on social media posting pictures of themselves helping the disadvantaged. One hand feeding the homeless, while the other is holding the phone taking a selfie. Is this an authentic, unconditional act of service?

What if we were to recognize that the path to living an authentic life is through our service to others? Yet our service has no limitations or exceptions. In behaving this way, our service is our reward, not the selfie, or the approval of those we are trying to help.

One of the things about service is we always associate it with grand events, housing every homeless person, ending world hunger, or quality medical care for all. These are wonderful goals that do demand our attention. But our service can also be as simple as helping someone cross the street, donating to our local food bank, or giving someone a bouquet of flowers. With this point of view, anything we do for others, with love as its foundation, would be considered an act of true service.

Many great spiritual teachings say the path to true enlightenment must go through acts of service. This opens the door to expressing our love for others, or the planet through our behavior. If there is a reward, it is our service, not the end result. By accepting this truth, we may become more conscious of the way we behave when we extend a helping hand to those in need.

I have seen people sacrificing their true happiness for others, thinking this is a loving act of service. Yet what about the love for oneself, because self-sacrifice is not an act of unconditional love. What if we first connected with the never-ending flow of love found deep within us, then shared this love through our service to others?

In living this way, we are not seeking admiration or recognition. We are of service because we know that the love at the core of our being expands when our service is unconditional and free from expectations. When our service is genuine and authentic, we will not be asking others for their approval. Our service will be founded on love, and it is this love that will generate well-being throughout the world.

Showing Up

How many times have we shown up for others, long before we showed up for ourselves? Do we care for them first because we are seeking their approval? Do we believe they will have something for us if we sacrifice ourselves to help them fulfill their desires? One of the biggest challenges we face in life is being fully engaged in our own journey. Do we take ourselves seriously? Are our needs met before we meet the needs of others?

If we take an honest look at our life, we recognize that no other person will do for us what we can do for ourselves. We cannot ask others to be the backbone we need when difficult times arise. It is important to show up for ourselves if we want to live an authentic life.

Being true to ourselves may be challenging. Through much of life we have been taught to seek the advice and support of those around us. In a way, we have learned we cannot trust our own inner wisdom, we must look for guidance outside of ourselves.

Has the advice of a close friend or parent been contrary to the direction we wanted to travel? If we choose to follow their suggestions, we will end up separated from our inner truth. Their wisdom may not be in harmony with what we know to be true and right for us. We are often too afraid to go in a direction that aligns with our truth because we do not want to disappoint those close to us.

Showing up for ourselves means we accept responsibility for the outcome of our choices. We know what we want even though others may not see our dreams as we do. We then move forward with a course of action that is in alignment with the truth of who we are. We may have to go it alone, but at least we are honoring our authentic self.

If we make a choice then stumble or fail, we remain emotionally centered, allowing ourselves to see the lessons we needed to learn at the time. We then use what we have learned to bolster our strength and courage to continue moving forward on our journey.

Of course some days will be tougher than others, but what will carry us through is knowing we are doing what we feel is authentic and true. When we have good days, we may get much accomplished, we may feel we are making up for the tough days. But at the end of every day, no matter how the day has turned out, if we do our work truthfully and honestly, we will know we have done our best by showing up for ourselves.

People often feel uncomfortable with those who march to their own drummer. Those who move through life to their own beat don't seem to fit in. They view the world differently, seeing opportunities where others see roadblocks. Their confidence arises from a knowledge of their true self. They know they are unstoppable when their goals align with the truth of who they are. Showing up for themselves is not an option, or a choice saved for good days. Showing up is a way through life, a journey to know their inner truth, who they are destined to become.

Those who show up for themselves know nothing is impossible and miracles take time. All it takes is placing one foot in front of the other. There is a knowing that the quality of the journey is the goal, not the final destination. There can be no doubt or negative self-talk. When this negativity does surface, it is quickly banished from the mind.

It cannot be expected that others will understand the choices we make. Only we know what is right for us. Yet we move through life knowing the advice of others comes from their experiences and their fears as well.

When we choose to show up for ourselves, we realize we may not find guidance that fits our needs. We also understand we cannot ask those who remain in their comfort zone what life is like beyond their point of view. They cannot see that far.

Showing up for ourselves takes tremendous courage and stamina. We must learn to trust ourselves when others doubt us. Our desire for a fulfilling life compels us to keep walking forward even though we cannot see the path clearly. On this authentic journey, fear becomes a teacher, rather than a deterrent.

As we begin the process of living to the fullness of who we are, we recognize that when times become difficult, and those close to us have fallen away, we will be the only voice encouraging us forward. Our faith in our ability to see how far we can go will carry us through bad times as well as good.

Showing up for who we are is the single greatest expression of self-love we will ever experience in our physical body. Yet it all begins with a desire to understand the truth of who we are, why we are here on Earth, and a commitment to share our life purpose with those around us.

Stillness

How often do we attain stillness in our busy lives? Do we find it in an evening walk, our morning meditation, or working out at the gym? If we can't find stillness in the outside world, can we find it within ourselves while we go through our daily routine?

One challenge many people face during meditation is silencing the mental chatter with the intention of finding a few moments of stillness. It's the constant stream of thoughts that prevents us from achieving our goal. Rather than trying to stop the flow of our thoughts, can we instead disconnect our involvement with them? Like letting go of a balloon, watching our thoughts float away without attachment to them.

If stillness is so elusive in our hectic world, can we live without it? Do we need to find stillness to live to the fullness of who we are? Yes, we do, because at the core of our being is an eternal source of everlasting love. This love speaks to us through our intuition. Yet we often cannot hear this loving voice because of the noise in our mind. As we work to arrive at a place of stillness, we will begin to hear and feel the wisdom of our intuitive guidance, leading us to the best life possible.

Stillness is a state of mind we can achieve through focus. One way to reach stillness is to recognize that which is worthy of our consideration and that which is not. Much of what is happening in the outside world may not require our attention.

Not every post on social media needs our approval, nor do we have to become emotionally involved in the drama we see around us. We can choose where to place our focus; this ability will help us enter into stillness easier.

When we are concentrating on certain tasks, we may notice moments of stillness. Even though writing demands my full attention, I am in a state of stillness, nothing matters other than the writing. In a way, writing quiets my mental chatter. This gives me the opportunity to clear my head of unwanted thoughts, while still being engaged.

Is it stillness if we are doing something that asks for our focused attention? Each of us will have to answer that question for ourselves. If we can quell the racket in our head by being focused, we will benefit emotionally.

Oftentimes artisans will find stillness while practicing their craft. They are focused on creating, allowing themselves to silence their inner noise so they can hear the voice of their authentic self, guiding them through the artistic process.

We do not have to produce great works of art to find stillness. We can focus on watching birds flying, snow falling, or listening to the sound of rain hitting the window. Observing nature is a good way to move into a state of stillness. Even watching waves of tall grass or the leaves of trees bending in the wind will offer us a few moments of stillness. These brief times of stillness will benefit us as much as sitting in meditation struggling to control our thoughts.

As we become more skilled at finding stillness, we begin to walk through life emotionally balanced. Our state of stillness will help us maintain our composure when challenges arise. It is here we learn to center ourselves before we react to unpleasant situations. Stillness offers us the wisdom to evaluate the circumstances before us, allowing us to respond in a manner beneficial to our well-being.

To realize our authentic self, finding moments of stillness must be incorporated into our daily practice. It makes no difference if we arrive at stillness in meditation, creating art, or observing nature. Our emotional health will improve because of these moments of inner calm.

T

Terrorize

We often allow the negative behavior of others to terrorize us. Yet do we notice when we give our thoughts the power to do the same? This may seem odd, but when we become aware of the harmful thoughts and ideas circulating in our head, we may indeed be our own terrorist.

Think of a time when failure was a part of our life. What self-destructive thoughts went through our mind? How long did those thoughts control our emotional state of being? Are we not strong enough to learn from our failures and move on?

Terrorizing ourselves because of past mistakes is a form of self-abuse. Do we dislike ourselves so much we have to reinforce our self-hatred by continually criticizing ourselves? Nothing positive comes from this self-defeating tendency.

If we dig deep, with the intention of understanding this negative behavior, we will notice a lack of self-compassion. Although the cause might be more severe, we may recognize we are living a life devoid of self-love. In the absence of love for ourselves, we have no defense against the terror of our own negative thinking.

I don't use the word terror lightly. Yet how often do we repeat harmful words to ourselves causing us to lose self-confidence? Is it because we believe that by speaking this way we will become a better person? How do we feel after a session listening to our inner terrorist?

The power of our words should never be underestimated. This includes the words we say to ourselves. It is not only our words that have the potential to terrorize us. The pain wrapped in a memory has the ability to separate us from our very own self-love.

Many of us have had painful experiences in life. Yet it is a choice to replay them over and over again in our mind. Could it be we are seeking a villain to blame? Or are we reliving the experience to answer our "Why?" As painful as it is, this behavior is easier than doing the inner work to learn and heal from the experience.

Do we forget that much of what we have swirling around in our head is there because we allow it to be there? We have the power to throw this junk out, just like taking trash to the dump.

It takes courage and strength to stand up to the thoughts terrorizing us each day. If we are seeking inner peace we must decide if a thought adds value to our life.

One method to evaluate a thought would be to question if it has a foundation of love. Are the things terrorizing us rooted in love? The majority of negative thoughts have no love in them. Yet we choose to keep them around because they may justify our anger and bitterness, even though they cause us great pain.

When I notice a thought terrorizing me, I ask myself, "Why am I thinking this thought, what purpose is it serving?" This gives me a moment to refocus my attention on anything more pleasant. I'll do whatever I can to shift my focus away from the negative thought. This helps me return to a healthier state of mind.

Often, we terrorize ourselves by expecting an apology from

those who caused us pain. We believe if they apologize, we will be liberated from the painful memory. Yet an apology is rarely given, and if one is expressed, it may not set us as free as we had hoped.

At some point self-forgiveness becomes an essential part of our healing. Forgiving ourselves gives us the ability to recognize that we are always doing the best we can. No matter what has happened to us in the past, we were doing our best.

This is not an excuse to behave poorly. It allows us to understand that given what we knew at the time we acted in the best way possible. Self-forgiveness gives us the courage to silence the terrorist of self-doubt and negative self-talk.

The best way to defeat the terrorist lurking in our head, is to begin the inner work of loving ourselves. Challenging our thoughts to see if love is at the root may not be easy but will aid in clearing away unhealthy thoughts and beliefs. Creating a gratitude list helps us recognize those things that have meaning, while adding value to our life.

These powerful tools give us the confidence to reconnect with our authentic self and align with the love at the core of our being. Thereby providing the awareness needed to overcome the terrorist hiding within our own mind.

Threshold

WHAT IF EACH OF US WAS standing at the threshold of knowing our true self? For some this is frightening, others may be unsure. Yet a small few, realize the life they have always wanted will be found on the other side of this threshold.

The catch is, once we step across the threshold, we can never go back, nor will we ever be the same. In the process we may lose friends, family members may disown us, causing us to feel alone on our journey.

Living to the fullness of who we are strips away anything that is not authentic from our being. We cannot walk over the threshold carrying our emotional baggage. We must leave it behind; it serves us no useful purpose.

As we walk forward, it's as if we are naked, bare of the thoughts and beliefs we once held as important. We now see how these thoughts and beliefs limited our ability to be honest with ourselves.

Crossing the threshold, our battle cry of self-righteousness falls silent as we realize the self-serving nature of our behavior. We cannot go forward carrying the banner advertising our victimhood. We must set it aside if our intention is to heal from the emotional wounds of our past.

Taking the first few steps on this journey, we are humbled by the love flowing through our being. We have never felt love this deeply. What we thought was love was bondage, chains keeping us attached to others. Unknown to us at the time, our love was a form of slavery. We used our behavior to manipulate others, trying to convince them it was love.

Stepping over the threshold, our choices will be based on love, and a desire to share this love freely, without the expectation of a reward. We love for the joy of loving. There are no more conditions or expectations. Love is the meaning of life. Sharing our love is a gift to the world.

Now, on the other side of the threshold, we recognize our imperfections, we see them without judgement. Our faults become the lessons we need to improve ourselves. Lessons we could not accept in the past.

We understand how our need to blame only harmed ourselves, limiting the way we experienced the world around us. The power of our blame hindered our growth, denying us the ability to live authentically.

After crossing the threshold, we realize our life is more compassionate, kind and loving. We have no reason to spread negativity, gossip, or hatred. We understand that love is the foundation of who we are. A lesson we could not comprehend on the other side of the threshold.

Although we may not see the path clearly, we know we are on the right path. Lead by our loving intuition we move forward knowing there will be guidance helping us along the way.

The fear we once knew, has passed. Our intuition leads us through life. We trust ourselves because we know ourselves better than anyone has ever known us. We do not need to seek advice from others. Their advice is based on their experiences. Many are too afraid to cross the threshold. Because of this, their opinions are outdated for our present state of life.

Each of us has the ability to step across this threshold, yet oftentimes we are too afraid of the life changes that will take place. There is no comfort zone once we cross over. Only the feeling of unconditional love. A love we have discovered within ourselves. A love we have been denying ourselves for far too long.

Walking further away from the threshold, deeper into the unknown, our confidence grows. We then begin to live truthfully. There is no need to try to fool ourselves into thinking we are living authentically as we have in the past. Our authenticity is a life founded on truth, love, and compassion.

Having crossed the threshold, we come face to face with the truth of who we are. The façade we once carried as protection is no longer needed. Our truth is the mantle we now wear. This truth tells people who we are before we even speak.

With time, Divine love fills our being, radiating from our body, and the world reacts to this love. It cannot be denied. This love is never-ending, it is eternal. There is no doubt when we experience this love, we know instinctively it is true, unquestionable.

Although the threshold is available to all, we must be courageous enough to take the first step if our intention is to live to the fullness of who we are. The journey may scare us, the unknowns are unpredictable, yet it will be the feeling of unconditional love that will persuade us to continue moving forward.

Triggers

What is it that sets us off? Are we courageous enough to examine the way we react to the challenges we face throughout our day? What if we noticed our triggers and then used this knowledge to heal and grow emotionally?

I get angry when my dog barks in the night. His barking is a trigger that controls me emotionally. This may seem crazy, he's just a dog. If I get upset at him for barking, what other situations trigger me?

We often think we are strong and balanced emotionally, although our triggers may be deeply rooted in our consciousness. When we learn to recognize our triggers, we can start the healing process of disconnecting ourselves from the power these triggers have over us.

This requires an honest look at our behavior because it can be easy to blame the cause of the trigger for the way things work out. But no true healing will take place if we choose the path of blame. What if we were to change our point of view and see our triggers as a step toward living a truly self-loving life?

The way to accomplish this would be to realize that our triggers are messages shining light on the areas of our consciousness that need work. Rather than get upset, we can ask ourselves, "What do we need to learn from our reactive behavior?" If we choose to live as we have been living, with blame becoming our go to emotion, then we are not being honest with ourselves. In behaving this way, we will be delaying any meaningful healing.

We could say we don't need healing because our triggers are just a part of life. But if the intention of life is to live to the fullness of who we are, then we must uncover the reasons why these triggers have prevented us from living an authentic life.

Noticing what triggers us is one of the many steps we must take if we want to live to our true potential. Think of triggers as a message guiding us along our journey to fulfillment. With each new reaction, we have an opportunity to learn something positive about ourselves, allowing us to move forward in a self-loving way.

If we choose to see our triggers as an opportunity for emotional growth, we will quickly move away from the negativity of anger when we *do* get triggered. With practice, we may even notice our triggers before we react, thereby remaining centered emotionally.

Some triggers arise within ourselves without much warning. Anxiety, the feeling of being overwhelmed, and worry, to name a few, are triggers that can reveal to us an underlying emotion in need of our attention. Often, these triggers cause us to lose our inner strength and may result in us falling back into old, unhealthy patterns.

Not all triggers have a negative effect on us emotionally. When I smell chocolate brownies baking, it triggers a childhood memory of enjoying my grandmother's brownies with a glass of milk on a cold winter day. Triggers like these can return us to a special time in our life.

Although, if we use our triggers as a way to escape life, then these triggers are doing us more harm than good. When we begin to understand why certain situations trigger us, whether it's the dog, a co-worker, or an emotional challenge at home, we can begin the healing process. By using our awareness of the causes of our triggers as a steppingstone, we can work our way toward a healthier life.

Truth

We often ask ourselves, "What is the truth?" The answer will be different for each of us because our definition of the truth will be based on our unique circumstances. Is it possible to arrive at a universal truth that would satisfy everyone?

Then we must ask, where will we find the truth, where do we begin? What if we were to consider the love found at the core of our being as the truth? The challenge then becomes one of uncovering this love.

Much of our life is spent changing who we are to please others. At a young age we were asked to behave in a way that would make our parents happy. From there, we changed who we were to make friends, then changed again to keep these friends or to fit in. As this cycle continues, changing our persona to adapt to the situation, we lose sight of who we are. Distancing ourselves from the unconditional love of our authentic truth.

Moving through life this way, we notice we are unhappy, but unsure why. Not much brings us lasting joy, and we feel disconnected from anything meaningful. Unhappy and unfulfilled, we search the outside world for something that will offer us a sense of worth, but to no avail. We realize the person we are and the life we are living is not what we had intended, asking ourselves, "How did we end up here?" As we scour the outside world for meaning, our authentic self is begging us to look within.

One way to begin the work of discovering the truth of who we are, is to ask if our thoughts, beliefs, and actions align with unconditional love. We may try to fool ourselves into thinking our negative behavior is justified, although negativity has no foundation of love.

Some would argue love has nothing to do with our truth, yet love is the energy of all creation. When we love without conditions or expectations, we are living a life of truth and honesty. Living a life of unconditional love aligns us with the truth of all creation. Living this way will also unite us with the love at the core of our being, thereby allowing us to live a life of truth.

How is this so? How does love align us with our truth? To love to the fullness of who we are, we must be honest. We cannot lie or push a negative agenda. Nor can we blame others for the way our life has unfolded. We must accept responsibility for our actions, yet we must also be responsible for our thoughts and beliefs.

To accept full responsibility for our life, past and present, we must be honest with ourselves. We must accept our mistakes, our misspoken words, our unfulfilled promises, as well as our biases and prejudices. Although at times painful to accept, these experiences draw us closer to the truth of our love for ourselves. If we attempt to deny our self-responsibility, we separate ourselves from the truth of who we are.

The more in depth we question ourselves, the more we shed thoughts and beliefs that limit the way we experience life. As our journey continues, we begin to feel a sense of love unlike any love we have witnessed before. Yet it all begins with being truthful with ourselves.

To live to the fullness of who we are, we must be loving in all aspects of our life. We cannot love halfway, claiming to be loving and kind, while hating a certain few. To live our truth, we love without conditions or expectations. We love freely without the need for a reward for the love we share.

This journey might seem difficult at times, yet the destination is a life founded on unconditional love, supported by an unwavering truth that cannot be denied. All this is available to us when we choose to look within ourselves for the truth we cannot find in the outside world.

Underlying

When we look at the architecture of ancient times, we will notice a solid foundation supporting the structure. This underlying material maintains the stability of whatever is built upon it.

What underlying structure do we have supporting us? Do we have a foundation of love? Or is our underpinning based on negativity? We may not think this is important, but when we realize we create a life based on our underlying emotions, our foundation does indeed matter.

Our underlying emotions are the building blocks for the life we choose to live. Yet our awareness of these emotions may be lacking. We often think our emotions are how we feel at any given time. In many cases this is true. Although underlying emotions may be hidden from view because of the pain they may hold within them.

There was a time when I was always angry. I did what I could to hide this from others, yet at times the anger came through. It wasn't until later in life I realized my anger was my baseline underlying emotion. In a way, anger was the foundation of the life I was creating.

It takes courage to journey within to uncover our underlying emotions. If we want to live an authentic life, we must do what we can to heal from the causes of this type of negativity.

Many underlying emotions settled within us when we were

children, through a traumatic experience. These negative emotions can resurface any time life becomes too challenging. Believing we are victims for example, is a powerful underlying emotion that will limit the way we express and accept love.

One way to uncover our underlying emotions would be to pay attention to the words we use. Much can be revealed when we listen to how we speak to others when difficulties arise. This awareness takes strength and courage, because we must be honest with ourselves when we recognize the basis for our everyday language.

Another way is to observe our life. Imagine stepping back and watching how we go through our day, and the interactions we have with others, examining how we treat those around us and then noticing how we react to their behavior toward us.

Are we loving, kind, and patient, or aggressive, defensive, or rude? Are we submissive, trying to remain unseen, passive because we don't want to make others upset? Do we believe the world is against us?

When we learn to accept that at the core of our being is a source of everlasting, unconditional love, we can use this love to heal ourselves from the wounds of a traumatic past.

We may not be able to do anything about the events of our history, yet we can begin the healing process through the loving act of self-forgiveness. Why self-forgiveness? Oftentimes when we go through a painful experience, we judge ourselves as not doing enough to stand up for ourselves.

In certain situations, we may carry the burden of shame or guilt. These emotions insulate us from feeling our own self-love. As we learn to forgive ourselves for holding onto this self-destructive behavior, we allow our self-love to fill our being, thereby healing any emotional wounds we may be harboring.

The intention is to clear away any negativity we are holding within our consciousness. This way our underlying emotions shift toward ones more positive, understanding, and thoughtful. From this place of positivity, our outlook will change, allowing our life experiences to reflect these loving emotions.

To live to the fullness of who we are, we must have a solid foundation of love. This way we can build a life that surpasses our wildest dreams. When we do encounter negativity, the strength of our positive underlying emotion will carry us through. From this emotional state of being, we will notice our life becoming kinder and more compassionate, as we begin to align with the truth of who we are.

Understanding

Wʜʏ ɪs ɪᴛ ᴡᴇ ᴅᴏ ɴᴏᴛ take the time to understand those who appear different from us? Is it because we are too insecure in our own self that we choose to judge instead of understanding? We could look at it this way, judgement lacks knowledge while understanding comes from a place of wisdom.

It takes courage to understand. We may have to set aside our preconceived ideas and false assertions to uncover the truth. When we choose to pigeonhole a person into our idea of who they are, we do so to make us feel better about ourselves. This limits our understanding of who they are.

Think of a time when you were judged without a clear understanding of who you were. How did that make you feel? All people want to be understood, yet for some reason we rely on inaccurate opinions and false beliefs to determine who a person might be.

To understand we must challenge the beliefs that prevent us from seeing the totality of a person. We may judge them on their accent, their clothes, even the food they eat. They may love or pray differently than we do, but we choose not to seek an honest understanding of the differences we have. Is it because we feel superior in our place of judgement?

By limiting challenging ideas from entering our consciousness, we hinder our ability to uncover the truth. We are too stuck in our beliefs to understand a different point of view.

When we lack understanding, we fail to grow emotionally and spiritually.

Much of how we view people and the world around us is based on our thoughts and beliefs. These are the foundations of who we are and how we interact with the outside world. We find comfort in our thoughts and beliefs because we rarely question if they advance our life or keep us in place.

The thing about becoming more understanding is we must question our thoughts and beliefs. Many of the ideas we hold true originated from the biases of other people. If our parents didn't like someone, we created a belief of not liking them as well.

As children we may have bullied the kid who looked different or spoke a foreign language. We acted this way because those around us behaved in a similar fashion. We didn't know any better. At that age we were too immature to take the time needed to understand those who appeared different from us.

The great thing about life is at any time we can choose to look deeper at that which we do not understand. All we have to do is find the courage to ask a question, then open our heart to hear the answer.

If the answer makes us uncomfortable, then that's a good thing. The discomfort is challenging us to seek more clarity. If the answers justify our negative thought process, then we are not asking the right questions.

The intention of asking these types of questions is to help us arrive at a place where we no longer need to judge others. When we understand, we are more likely to be sincere with those who appear different.

True understanding allows us to consider another point of view with the issues that challenge us. This gives us the flexibility to change our opinion if needed, thereby opening the door to an understanding lacking in prejudice.

As we access the courage needed to be understanding, we become more accepting of those who appear different from us. We may realize our judgement was baseless. Knowing each of us might be working to overcome unseen challenges gives us the opportunity to open our heart to those who view the world differently than we do.

Arriving at an emotional state of understanding gives us the ability to see people clearly, without the negativity of our judgement or false beliefs clouding our view. It is here we have the compassion to allow the truth of a person to be recognized and accepted.

Unique

YOU ARE UNIQUE IN EVERY WAY. No one thinks like you, expresses themselves as you do, nor is it possible for any other person to affect the world as you do. You are uniquely you, there is no doubting your uniqueness.

Yet if we are unique, why do we try to fit into a box that will make society comfortable? Even our family would like us to remain in their preconceived ideas of who they think we should be.

Oftentimes we want to be liked and accepted by others so badly we change who we are to please them. Our thought is, if we change in a certain manner, they may show their love for us. In behaving this way, we sacrifice our uniqueness for the superficial affection of others.

The question becomes, "What about our love for ourselves?" When we downplay our uniqueness to please others, we are denying the world our inner truth. By depriving those around us of our uniqueness we are cheating ourselves out of the love found at the core of our being.

When we begin to live by the power of our self-love, we have no reason to change who we are. We realize there is no need to adjust our point of view to fit into a neat little box constructed by others. Our self-love is the foundation of who we are, and our uniqueness is the way we share this love.

At times our uniqueness may challenge those in our life. It

is not our responsibility to muffle who we are to gain acceptance or make others comfortable. It is the responsibility of society to ask why our uniqueness bothers them.

Those who are connected to the love found at the core of their being will accept our uniqueness. They are not threatened by those who appear different. Although certain aspects of our uniqueness may cause others to hesitate, they do not judge because they know that everyone is doing the best they can in searching for their inner truth.

Our uniqueness is a gift we share without conditions or expectations. We recognize the uniqueness in others, yet we have no need to judge, or ask anyone to align with our way of viewing life. Thereby allowing others the freedom to live to the fullness of who they are.

Each of us comes from a different place emotionally, physically, and spiritually. This gives us the resources needed to accomplish great things when we choose to work together. Although it is essential to look within ourselves for guidance rather than asking others for an opinion that may not benefit us. To live to the fullness of who we are, we must learn to trust ourselves, no matter how many people doubt us.

Throughout much of life we have been taught to fall in line and obey the rules while keeping quiet. For some, this type of life brings a sense of comfort. Yet for those who have acknowledged their uniqueness, living this way is not possible. They have a different perspective on life and intend to share it with the world.

Those who accept their uniqueness are courageous enough to challenge the ideas of remaining within a comfort zone. They see the limitations of comfort, choosing not to live by the rules set forth by the fear of the unknown.

In a sense, living by our uniqueness sets us free. We realize there is no point in trying to please everyone, or changing who we are just to fit in. We are free from seeking the opinions of others because we trust our ability to look within ourselves to find the emotional support we once sought from the outside world.

Yet this is not about us versus them, because each of us is unique. When we live to the fullness of who we are, we allow others the freedom to discover their uniqueness as well. We know that through the journey of self-discovery we arrive at the doorway to our authentic self. This is the path to living a fulfilling life, yet this journey will be difficult if we hide the gift of our uniqueness from the world around us.

Unknown

IF OUR INTENTION IS TO LIVE to the fullness of who we are, we must walk into the unknown. Nothing of any value will come from our comfort zone. Sitting on the couch wishing for life to change will lead us nowhere. As scary as the unknown may be, it is where we will discover the truth of who we are.

When we begin the journey to reconnect with our authentic self, we must open the door to the unknown. We may be frightened, we may be unsure, but to see how far we can go, we must accept that the path to a fulfilling life goes through the unknown.

The interesting thing about the unknown is we will gain a level of confidence as we journey deeper and deeper away from the security of our comfort zone. With each new experience, we will tap into previously unknown skills, unlock higher levels of wisdom, thereby shifting our mindset toward what is possible.

The unknown can stifle our growth or energize us to accomplish great things. It will all depend on our ability to adapt to the ever-changing landscape. As we journey into the unknown, we will have to develop the strength to quiet our self-doubt, ignore our negative self-talk, and shed our limiting beliefs. Our mind will be our best friend or our worst enemy. It will all hinge on how well we can remain focused on our dreams and goals.

There will be other distractions as well. Those around us will express their doubt, causing us to question ourselves. Although they may claim to love us, their advice may serve no useful purpose. The unknown scares them, causing them to project their fears onto us.

If we are aware of the possibilities in the unknown, we will learn something beneficial every day. Each challenge holds within it a lesson we need to help carry us forward. It may sound crazy, but the unknown may become our best ally. In the darkness of the unknown, those who doubt us will have been left behind. All we will have is ourselves and the knowledge that we are on the right path.

As we travel further into the unknown, we realize the success of our journey will be based on the choices we make. We understand that our successes and failures are our responsibility. There is something comforting in knowing we are in control of our destiny.

If we succeed, it will be because we believed in ourselves and took the chance. If we fail, we have no shame, we tried, hopefully we gave it our best shot. But we always have a choice to get up, brush off the dirt, learn what we can, and continue on, or wallow in our failure. No matter the outcome we have no reason to blame others, we have no reason to blame ourselves. In failure, the unknown has taught us an important lesson.

Life can be challenging, this is why it is so easy to remain in place, continuing a comfortable routine. How will we feel when we have little time left here on Earth? Will we regret the chances we didn't take, the words we should have spoken, the comfort that chained us in place? Will we be bitter because we chose to accept our fear as a way of life to avoid the unknown?

Or will we look back at the struggles we overcame while surrounded by the unknown and express gratitude for the growth of our consciousness and the life we lived? With each new day we have the opportunity to live to the fullness of who we are, but to do so, we must face the unknown, to see what rewards it holds for us.

Victim

THE OUTCOME OF OUR LIFE WILL be determined by the choices we make. We have a choice. Focus on the inconvenience of the rain or focus on the benefits of the rain. Whether the rain or the pain we hide from others, we get to choose where we place our attention.

Our focus will attract similar energy back to us. If we choose to place our attention on the pain we have suffered at the hands of others, that energy will continue to circulate in our consciousness, affecting the way we experience life. Although if we realize our emotional health is our responsibility, we can take the steps necessary to begin the healing process.

The challenge begins when we realize we must forgive before healing can take place. Rather than forgive, we choose to play the role of the victim. As we accept this role, we solidify our connection with the person who caused our pain. We may never break free from them or the pain when we choose the victim mentality.

If we look closer, we notice we have the freedom to make choices for our well-being. Choosing to forgive elevates us away from the negativity surrounding our pain, while choosing victimhood bonds us to this negativity.

As time goes by, our role as the victim becomes our identity. All those in our life have heard of our pain, yet we continue to reinforce this narrative with every new opportunity.

When we repeat the story that caused our pain, we do so to boost our sense of worth, hoping those who hear our tale will sympathize with us, adding energy to our fragile persona. Fragile, because we have built an image of ourselves based on negativity and our desire for others to accept us through the stories we share, strengthening our role as a victim.

We fail to realize their acceptance hinders our ability to begin the inner work needed to help us move away from our role as a victim. Our resistance to heal arises from the questions, "Who are we if we are not the victim?" "What will we have if we walk away from our victim identity?"

Choosing the victim label, we deny ourselves the love found at the core of our being. This love loves us regardless of what happened in the past and will love us no matter what happens in the future.

By sharing the stories that cause us to play the victim, we distance ourselves from this source of unconditional love. We create a persona that matches our pain and suffering, not an identity that aligns with the truth of who we are.

We can change our focus anytime. All we must do is realize we are missing much of what our authentic self has to offer. When we notice that our victim mentality limits the way we experience life, we can begin to do the work of connecting with our truth.

Although it might be difficult to forgive, the truth of who we are will be found on the path of forgiveness. It is in this place of power and strength we realize we have always been doing the best we could. The ability to forgive gives us the opportunity to move away from a persona that did us more harm than good.

We may ask why we should forgive; we did nothing wrong.

In some cases, this may be true. Yet we can also forgive ourselves. Oftentimes there is shame and guilt associated with our pain. Through the loving act of self-forgiveness, we free ourselves from the pain as well as our victim persona.

If we are courageous enough to seek total freedom from our role as a victim, we can choose to forgive our assailant for the pain they have caused. Although challenging, this type of forgiveness is a powerful act of self-love.

We forgive others because we love ourselves enough to separate ourselves from them and the pain they have caused. One thing to remember is we do not have to see them or speak to them to forgive. We can forgive, then move on without having their presence reignite a painful memory.

When we realize the success of our life will depend on the choices we make, we understand that forgiveness is a choice we cannot delay. Once we reconnect with the unconditional love found at the core of our being, we will discover the courage and self-worth to reject our victim persona.

Victories

We often think of landing a high paying job, buying a fancy car, or owning a luxury home, as a victory. In some cases, it is. Yet do we ever consider the challenges and roadblocks we have overcome as victories? Do our victories have to be validated by others, or can they be private? It feels wonderful when we accomplish a goal that we can share with those around us. What about our smaller victories, those having value only to us?

Why is it we overlook the victories that appear unimportant? For some, getting out of bed can be a victory while others do their best to keep their addiction at arms-length. These are victories, no matter how insignificant we think they are. Celebrating these accomplishments can help boost our self-confidence.

We will have moments in life when there is no one nearby to support us emotionally. Even though we may be struggling, we need to become our own cheerleader to encourage ourselves on to victory. The ability to pick ourselves up and keep moving forward after getting knocked down reveals to us how resilient we are when life becomes difficult.

The world is full of distractions, pulling our attention away from the present moment. In certain situations these distractions may benefit us emotionally. While other times they cause us to lose focus, even forcing us to question our ability to keep moving forward. This is why celebrating our small victories is important.

It may not seem like much, but when we recognize our victories, we give ourselves a boost of positive energy. It makes no difference what scale the victory may be, a win is a win. Each small victory helps build momentum. If we understand the phrase, "The journey of a thousand miles begins with a single step," then each step is a victory.

Every time we ignore an impulse to return to old, unhealthy behavioral patterns, we score a victory. Choosing to remain quiet when in the past we would have screamed in anger, is a victory. Setting our phone aside to have a conversation with a loved one, or finding a quiet moment for ourselves, is a victory. The list of unappreciated victories could go on forever.

With each victory we step closer to the truth of who we are. It can be too easy to remain in our comfort zone, too afraid to challenge ourselves to see what we can accomplish. When we realize life is for the living, we begin to take small chances which will lead to greater things. Each tiny risk gives us the opportunity to celebrate a victory.

If we fall flat on our face, failing miserably, at some level this is a victory. Why? Because we tried! We got off the couch, (which could be a victory in itself) left our comfort zone, (another victory) and ventured into the unknown (definitely a victory).

Even though we may have failed, the experience will teach us the lessons we need to succeed in the future. Recognizing the lessons in our failure is a victory. In doing so we separate ourselves from the anguish of failure, stepping aside and noticing what we needed to learn from the situation.

Whenever we turn toward a more positive way of thinking

and behaving, we should consider it a victory. The negativity of the outside world has the ability to draw us in, sucking the energy out of us. Choosing to remain centered when negative things happen is a victory.

Rather than accepting what our self-doubt and negative self-talk have to say, we can silence these voices with the intention of hearing the voice of our true self. Walking this path is a victory that will motivate us to keep moving forward toward a more fulfilling life.

As we begin the journey of uncovering our authentic self, we notice how our small victories boost our courage, stamina, and self-worth. It is these accomplishments that become the foundation of our successes, yet we must first acknowledge them as victories.

Villains

As we journey to live an authentic life, we notice many of our behavioral patterns may no longer serve our best interests. Among other things, is our need to label those who hurt us as "villains." When we identify a person or group of people as villains, we do so to avoid our self-responsibility. It is too easy to blame the villain. Accepting responsibility for our emotional health takes work, work we would rather avoid.

Yet if we choose to find a scapegoat for our problems, we may never heal from the wounds no one else can see. The wounds we choose to hide. By acting this way, we fail to realize the true villain may be looking back at us in the mirror.

To live a fulfilling life, it is best to release the villain from our consciousness. The villain, if we refuse to set them free, will control us emotionally whether they are alive or long gone.

The interesting thing about villains is we have criteria for these people. At some point even our closest friend will upset us. We love them, so setting them free is easy. When we select a villain, they are special. They may have accomplished something we have not. It's possible they hurt us without knowing it, yet they claimed to love us, causing the pain to cut deeper. At times our anger toward them is often filled with jealousy or resentment.

It seems nothing our villain does pleases us, no matter how many times they try to apologize, we ignore their plea. We hold the villain in an emotional prison, this prevents us from examining our own behavior. We point to the villain when life becomes difficult, because at some level we have a need to maintain our attention on their actions.

Our villain is so hated, we try to convince others to see this person as we do. Some people, those not in alignment with their true selves, may choose to accept the negative opinion of who the villain is.

Although those who are living by the love found at the core of their being will not see the villain the same way, thereby questioning our reasons for labeling this person as a villain in the first place.

Yet it all comes down to us. Why do we need a villain in our life? Is it because we are too afraid to turn our gaze inward to recognize our negative habits or actions? Do we fail to examine if we are loving and kind? Is it possible we are villains in the lives of others?

Answering these questions truthfully will reveal to us if the label of villain has merit, or just makes us feel superior. To live to the fullness of who we are it is essential to question any negative thought or belief we hold within our consciousness. In this place of self-examination we uncover the truth behind the reasons we judge others as villains.

When we choose to see others as villains, we refuse to begin the healing process. We like the label of villain. It gives us a reason to remain angry. Also, we hope it makes us look good in the eyes of others. While many times few people question why we are behaving this way.

If people do question our behavior, we accuse them of siding with the villain, thereby alienating those who view the villain differently. This negative behavior could spiral out of control, leaving us alone because we have accused those close to us of favoring the villain.

Taking an honest look at our behavior, we notice we may have had a role to play in the incident that caused us to label the villain. If we want to live a fulfilling life, moving toward our authentic truth, questioning our beliefs is essential.

As we work to release the negativity surrounding our judgement, we come closer to a loving state of mind. With love becoming the foundation of our life we accept responsibility for our actions. It is here forgiveness becomes the road to our healing.

Through the self-loving act of forgiveness, we realize our villain is doing the best they can. We understand our behavior is a form of judgement, intended to protect us from further pain. Yet our negative behavioral patterns will only move us away from the truth of who we are, preventing us from seeing the world through the eyes of love and compassion.

Vulnerability

Of all the emotions we face throughout life, being vulnerable might be the most difficult to master. We want people to know our truth, but fear being hurt emotionally. In the past we may have revealed a deep-seated pain, only to learn later what we thought was a moment of vulnerability had been used to wound us.

After this happens we choose to remain silent, locking our pain within our consciousness. At times keeping quiet is easier than sharing what is bothering us. The pain we hold within eats at us, destroying our inner peace, causing our anger to smolder unseen, while our self-worth crumbles.

Knowing who we can and cannot express our deepest feelings with is the challenge of being vulnerable. In our desire to be liked and accepted, we may speak to anyone who will listen to our story. Thinking this is a good thing, we end up revealing too much to the wrong people. It's wonderful to be vulnerable, but we must be cautious with whom we share our history.

Many people want us to be vulnerable, yet they are not willing to accept this responsibility. Our pain may be too great for them to bear. Or they may be the reason we have been hurt. Oftentimes those who ask us to be vulnerable are not capable of being vulnerable themselves.

Harboring our pain and regret is unhealthy. This negative energy will manifest in physical disease. Yet if all we are doing is sharing our pain without the intention of healing, we are just bragging.

Being vulnerable is an important part of the healing process. We must be open to sharing, yet we must allow the guidance beneficial to our well-being to be heard as well. True vulnerability is a balance between sharing and receiving.

One of the biggest challenges we face when we are asked to be vulnerable is whether we feel emotionally safe or not. The same is true for those we ask to be vulnerable with us. Have we created a safe environment in which we can express our vulnerability? If we do not feel safe, no amount of coercion will get us to show our raw, unprotected self.

As we begin the process of opening our true self to the world, we may withdraw at the slightest hint of abuse. This will cause us to hesitate if we are asked to reveal our truth in the future.

Shielding our vulnerability from the outside world will make it challenging to achieve meaningful relationships. Any we do have will be superficial, barely scratching the surface of who we are and what it means to live an authentic life.

The walls we build to protect our vulnerability grow stronger with time. It becomes easier to hide than it would be to expose our true self. Our fear of getting hurt by those we assume we can trust will force us to limit the way we express ourselves. Although not representative of our true self, our relationships will be built on this shallow façade.

The way to achieve authentic vulnerability is through the love found at the core of our being. When we learn to love ourselves, we open the door to being vulnerable. Yet we also allow others the freedom to be vulnerable as well. Knowing our words will not be used against us, we feel comfortable expressing ourselves.

Vulnerability is the pathway to living to the fullness of who we are. In this place of exposure, we allow the world to see our inner truth. We may fear being vulnerable, but our self-love gives us the courage and strength to overcome any difficulties that may arise.

In our powerful state of vulnerability, we love ourselves enough to know that if our truth is abused by others, we can safely walk away. We have no need for those who exploit the privilege of knowing our authentic self. If expressing our truth makes others uncomfortable or confrontational, we know this reflects the struggles they are facing.

Our challenge is to love ourselves enough so we can learn the lessons vulnerability teaches. In this wisdom, we find that being vulnerable allows us to love ourselves and others without conditions or expectations. We also realize that the truth of who we are will be discovered in our ability to be vulnerable, no matter the circumstances.

Walk

THROUGHOUT THE COURSE OF LIFE WE may have heard, "Tough it out," "It's your problem, not mine," or "This is all your fault." We do what we can to adjust our way of life to please those who spoke those words, yet it may cause us more suffering than we can handle.

Constantly hearing words such as these, we begin to crumble under the pressure of having to adopt an unhealthy narrative. In time we arrive at a point where our only option is to walk away. Although we think we have failed, walking away may be the best thing we could do for our emotional health.

We walk away for many reasons. One would be, we do not feel safe to say what is on our mind. The reaction to our words is neither accepting nor supportive. Often times when we do speak up, our words are used against us, accusing us of being the cause of the problem. It is here we learn that few people are willing to accept responsibility for their harmful behavior; blaming us is much easier.

Some would say walking away is a sign of weakness. Those who believe this do not understand the courage it takes to walk away from an unhealthy situation. When we choose to walk it is because we have hit rock bottom. Not having the stamina to deal with the situation any longer, walking seems to be the only choice.

One of the many reasons we choose to walk away would be

because we have been asked to change who we are to please others. We do what we can to change with the expectation of acceptance and a feeling of love being shown to us, although this rarely happens.

As we continue to change, we hope that through our metamorphosis we will feel a sense of value from those who are asking us to change. If we are trying to live an authentic life, we realize that no matter how much we change, we will never be accepted for who we truly are. In this case, walking away is the best thing we can do for our emotional stability, thereby giving us the opportunity to rediscover our true self.

It can be painful to walk away. We may have to leave people we love behind. We are too afraid, emotionally fragile, or hurt, to continue sharing our point of view. The pain is still there, yet we do not feel safe expressing ourselves. The fear of being verbally or physically abused encourages us to remain silent. Walking away becomes the only safe option.

We may not understand it at the time but walking away is an act of self-love. We realize we cannot remain in a toxic situation or relationship any longer, so we walk. We love ourselves enough to seek a healthier life. A life where we are not afraid to speak our truth, where those around us are accountable for their actions and are genuine in their concern for our overall well-being.

A thought to remember, when we walk away, we are walking toward something better. We may not see it at that moment, but by walking we have decided that what is before us, even though it may be unknown, is better than staying in place.

There will be those who will judge us harshly when we walk. We cannot concern ourselves with their opinion. People who judge may have no idea of the pain or suffering we have experienced. They will tell us to try to work through it, forgive and forget. Although this advice may make them comfortable, they do not have a clear picture of what we have endured.

By choosing to walk we may lose friends and family members may turn against us. Because of this we may feel isolated. Yet when we step away from those who harmed us, we open the door to new, healthier opportunities.

There will be a time when we will be strong enough to look over the past and learn from these experiences. We notice when we should have spoken up for ourselves. Or moments when it would have been beneficial to express our disappointment at how others were treating us. The strength to move forward will be found in these lessons.

The best we can do for ourselves is to learn from the past without dwelling on it. Our future is before us. When we decide to walk away from toxic situations or relationships that don't recognize our value, we do so because we love ourselves enough to seek a more fulfilling way of life.

Warrior

ALTHOUGH WE MAY NOT HAVE FOUGHT in a war, we often fight an unseen foe each and every day. If our intention is to overcome the challenges we face, we must summon the warrior within to do battle with these difficulties.

We often forget that the path to our authentic self is littered with challenges. These situations hold within them the important lessons we need to live in alignment with our inner truth. When we are faced with a challenge, we have two basic choices, fight through or give up.

The success of our journey depends on the amount of courage and stamina we can access. The thing about living an authentic life is it takes work that only we can do for ourselves. No other person can do this for us. In a sense, we must be a warrior fighting for what we know to be true and right for us.

Often times people will place blame on others for the way life has unfolded. This behavior ignores the responsibilities needed to live a life of truth, love, and kindness. We blame others because taking responsibility for our life is too frightening. That would mean where we are right now is our responsibility. In this state of acceptance we have no one to blame.

The thing about being a warrior is we may be frightened, hesitant, or full of self-doubt. Yet we carry on, even with this kind of negativity trying to hold us back. If we continue fighting for ourselves the chains keeping us in our comfort zone will break. Although when we step away from the life we find comfortable, we come face to face with a part of ourselves we may never have experienced in the past.

All warriors wear armor and carry a quiver of weapons, including our intuition, inner truth, the ability to see past our limiting beliefs, and the courage to remain true to ourselves. The armor protecting our warrior is built out of self-love. These weapons may be nonphysical, yet their power should never be underestimated.

The warrior knows the ego is always working to take control. We also recognize the ego is threatened by our authentic self. As we continue our journey to discover the truth of who we are, we must be vigilant against any attempt to derail our intention.

It is not only the battle within, where we need to be our own warrior. The physical world has many opportunities to throw us off center. Those who claim to love us will express their doubt and their negative opinions, even try to talk us out of walking an authentic path.

We must remain focused on the goal of realizing our true self, even if it makes others uncomfortable. This is not to say we don't love them, we do, but we must be willing to walk away from those who want to keep us in the box they have built for us.

Could it be our journey makes them feel awkward when they are with us? It may force them to reflect on how their life is unfolding, causing them to question themselves. Because of this, they may not want to see us achieve our goals.

Our inner warrior has a heart filled with love. We know that love heals, as well as conquers. There is no need to act out of anger or revenge. These negative emotions separate us from the love found at the core of our being. Love enriches the warrior from within, asking us to love without conditions, expectations, or judgements.

Living this way, we guide our life in a manner that benefits those we interact with throughout the course of the day. The only weakness our warrior may face is the comfort of returning to the way we once were. Our strength is love, and it is this love that will help us overcome any battle we face. Whether the conflict is in the physical world, or the inner realm of our own mind, our warrior will prevail as long as love is the weapon of choice.

What If?

WHAT IF WE TURNED LEFT INSTEAD of right? What if we had spoken the words rather than remained silent? What if we had chosen to journey into the unknown instead of taking the safe route? What if it turns out better than we could possibly imagine? What if the answer is yes?

"What if?" is a question both terrifying and exciting to answer. It will reveal to us if we are pessimists or optimists. Do we focus on what could go wrong, or do we see the unlimited possibilities available to us?

If we are intent on living an authentic life, we must ask ourselves "What if?" It takes courage to answer this question honestly, because we often form the answer in a way that makes us comfortable. Does answering the question this way do us any good?

What if we are wrong, or things turn out better than we expected? Our behavior will determine the outcome. If we choose to do nothing, then the answer will always be no. Yet if we show up as our authentic self, the answer will benefit us. Even if life falls apart, we know we will have done our best.

Asking "What if? puts the spotlight on our thoughts and behavior, because we must take responsibility for the outcome of our actions. What if they say yes? What if we are meant to accomplish great things, but sitting on the couch doing nothing makes us comfortable? "What if?" causes us to look within to see what possibilities exist.

When we ask, "What if?" it can be easy to list all the negative things that could happen. Yet we could easily list all the positive things as well. Asking "What if?" is a great way to uncover our limiting beliefs. If we are afraid, our answers will be fear based.

The intention of asking "What if?" is to sift through our beliefs that do not serve our best interests. Beliefs that limit the way we experience life must be challenged to see if we should release them from our consciousness. Once this cleansing begins, we will notice our energy changing, moving away from negativity to a more positive outlook.

What if we were to believe those who doubt us, those who are finding comfort in their limiting belief? Would we be happy living by the opinions of others? The truth of who we are will be found within us, yet we must have the courage to look inside ourselves to uncover this truth.

As we journey on the road toward discovering our authentic self, we must ask ourselves what if our truth is different than who we portray to the world? This alone may stop us from continuing on, but is this fair to ourselves? Are we willing to deny ourselves the truth of who we are because it might be different than who we show to the world?

To live an authentic life is why we are here on Earth. We are not meant to hide behind a manufactured persona because it pleases others, making them comfortable. Asking "What if?" opens the door to solving the mystery of who we are.

Imagine asking ourselves "What if we are destined to accomplish great things?" We may ask, "Why me?" The true answer will always be, "Why not me?" "What if?" helps us get to the bottom of our beliefs that don't benefit us. What if we are limiting the way we go through life because we don't want to challenge ourselves too much?

When I first began writing, I asked, "What if no one reads anything I write?" I could not allow that question to stop me. My self-worth was strengthened by the writing. The self-discovery was in doing the work, even though I had never done anything like that before. The growth came from realizing I could do whatever I set my mind to.

In a way, asking "What if?" gave me the courage to carry on. Rather than ask, "What if no one reads my work?" I asked, "What if everyone reads my writing?" Connecting with our authentic self is about moving past limiting beliefs and seeing what possibilities exist.

"What if?" gives us the ability to recognize the boundaries we have created that prevent us from living a successful life, while giving us the wisdom to break through these barriers.

As long as we are afraid to ask, "What if?" we will never know our true potential. Yet by asking this question, we begin the process of moving in a direction that just might give us the best life possible.

Wrong

It takes courage to confess when we are wrong. It might be too shameful for us to admit our mistakes, so we keep arguing that we are right. Yet how does this make us feel? If we refuse to acknowledge we are wrong, then how open minded are we?

To admit we are wrong takes inner strength and self-confidence. We must accept that we are not perfect, or that others may have more knowledge than we do. The challenge begins when we believe we know everything while anyone who doubts us is wrong.

Looking closer at our behavior, we notice we act as we do because we have a desire to be seen as an expert or authority. Someone who has had a vast life experience, someone who can be trusted. In a way, our self-worth is attached to how impressed others are with the wisdom we share.

Yet this leaves little room for seeing points of view that differ from our beliefs. When someone disagrees with us, we take it as a personal insult. We fail to recognize it as an opportunity to learn from the experience.

As we shed our ego persona and begin to live to the fullness of who we are, we come to the realization there is much we have yet to learn. In the course of living an authentic life, it is important to seek knowledge and wisdom, even if it contradicts our beliefs. This is where our emotional growth will be found.

How will we learn anything if we think we are always right? Do we refuse to look at our own behavior and question what we believe to be true? What may be wrong for us, may be right for others.

Each of us has a different life history. These are the experiences that shape the way we walk through our day. No two people will ever experience the same life changing event the same. If we truly believe this, is anyone wrong? This can be a challenge to accept because there are some basic truths in life. Yet at times even these truths will be called into question.

If our intention is to live to the fullness of who we are, we must learn to question our beliefs to see if they are valid, or if we are only repeating unhealthy patterns of thought. This can be difficult because our thoughts create our beliefs, and our beliefs shape our view of the world around us.

Self-examination can be hard on us emotionally because in our point of view, our beliefs have always been right. When we contemplate that our beliefs may be wrong, our foundation begins to shake. No matter how challenging it may be for us, examining our thoughts and beliefs is the right thing to do if we want to live an honest life.

Questioning ourselves may cause some discomfort, but in the long run it will be worth it. Our emotional health and well-being will benefit from releasing the thoughts and beliefs that do not serve our higher good. Yet our journey to living an authentic life is our responsibility. Once we begin walking this path, there is no need to prove others wrong, or boast about how right we are.

It all starts with accepting that we may be wrong when we judge others because they do not fall in line with our beliefs. By silencing our need to be right, we notice we can learn something from those around us. It is in this state of acceptance we begin to see how harmful it can be to our relationships when we deny we were ever wrong in the first place.

Xerox

Wʜᴇɴ ᴡᴇ ᴛʜɪɴᴋ ᴏғ Xᴇʀᴏx ᴡᴇ think of a machine that makes copies from an original. The question I have is, are we copies or are we original? It's easy to take on the beliefs and attitudes of those who influence our lives. But are we honest with ourselves to think and behave as an original?

Being a copy is easy. We don't have to challenge ourselves into thinking any differently than what we have been taught. We just mimic these lessons, hoping we are accepted by those around us.

Originality causes us to question many of our thoughts and beliefs. This can be difficult because we may begin to see the world differently from those who claim to love us. These differences have the potential to alienate us from those we love.

Living an original life takes stamina. It seems at every turn the world is trying to shape us into something we are not. If we are aligned with our originality, we remain true to ourselves. Yet if we are insecure, lacking self-worth, we may be forced into a life that separates us from our true self.

To live to the fullness of who we are, we must walk our own path. We cannot copy the behavioral patterns of others, expecting the world to accept us as original.

Our journey to live an authentic life is a solo journey. No one can walk it for us, or with us, we must do this work ourselves. On this journey we will be challenged by the roadblocks life puts in our way. How we handle these obstacles will reveal the truth of who we are, thereby determining the quality of our life.

The tough thing about the world today is many of the people we admire may not be original. Yet if we want to live a truthful life, it is important to find those who are. Not with the intention of copying them, but to learn how they navigate the challenges of life. We can use their originality as motivation when those around us want us to be someone we are not.

Being original does not mean we have to look outrageous. We can be as simple, or as complex as we want. As long as we live by the truth of who we are, we are not copies. Yet finding our truth is one of the biggest challenges we face in life.

The amazing thing about this world is the abundance surrounding us. We can be, do, or have anything we set out to accomplish. But that can also be a problem. When there are too many options, we become overwhelmed, unsure what choices to make. How do we know if something is right for us, or a distraction?

To be original, we may lose touch with our authentic self. We may go through many personas before we discover our truth. Just look around, the options are endless. We can lose focus with all the distractions thereby never reaching our goal of being original.

How will we know if we are on the right path to realizing our authentic originality? Deep within us is an unlimited source of unconditional love. As we align with the truth of who we are, we tap into this powerful source of love.

When we seek the approval of others to boost our self-esteem we disconnect from this love. To know if we are original, we must align with this love in every aspect of our life experience. As we learn to connect with this flow of love, we become aware of the voice of our intuition. It is this voice that guides us toward our authentic self.

As we go through life, we often seek the opinions of others for guidance. Their advice may not resonate with us, but to please them we abide by it anyway. By following this type of guidance, we ignore the voice of our true self. We are instead copying the suggestions of others rather than trusting what we know to be true and right for us.

Intuition is the voice of our authentic self. It is this guidance that leads us toward a life based on the truth of who we are. Yet this life will only happen when we make the decision to be true to ourselves by being original.

Xenodochial

THE WORLD IN WHICH WE LIVE is an amazing place. With so much variety, we could spend an entire lifetime traveling the globe experiencing different traditions. But the only way we can do this is if we are curious and "xenodochial." Being a xenodochial person means we are friendly and welcoming toward people of different cultures and backgrounds.

Why is it we think the only way to live is the way we live, or the best food is the food we eat? As long as we remain in our own little world, we will never realize the diversity around us. This means that to elevate our awareness we must travel outside our area.

A question to ask ourselves before we embark on a journey to explore the world is, are we a xenodochial type of person? If we are not interested in meeting new people or enjoying the local cuisine, then traveling abroad may be challenging.

It's easy to become comfortable with our surroundings. We know the layout, our favorite shops and restaurants are nearby, and we know the people we meet along the way. There is little that makes us feel awkward.

Moving away from what is familiar causes a certain level of uneasiness. Yet in these feelings we learn much about who we are. Meeting new and different people forces us to look within ourselves to challenge our beliefs toward the world around us.

Have we forgotten that we are one people on a spinning ball of rock in the middle of nowhere? Can we see others as brothers and sisters, even though they speak a different language? What if the meaning of life is to get along with those who view the world differently than we do?

Is it possible to agree that each of us has a unique point of view? That the beliefs of others have merit based on their culture? Being a xenodochail person is a person who accepts the diversity of the planet we inhabit.

We cannot claim to be in alignment with our authentic self if we limit our love to only those who look and sound like us. If we are true to ourselves, our love cannot have limitations or conditions.

Oftentimes our beliefs are so strong we fail to accept solutions presented by a culture different than our own. Yet to be an active member of the human race, we must look beyond national borders to find answers to the problems that commonly plague all people.

There may be those who never accept who we are. Yet how we interact with them will determine the success of our time here on Earth. Even if they cannot accept us, we can do our best to recognize their value in elevating global consciousness. This is where we learn that everyone is a teacher while at the same time understanding that we are students as well.

Setting aside our stereotype of foreigners, we realize we can learn something from each other. We begin the process of noticing our commonalities. Instead of seeing what separates us, we can look for what unites us.

Not all people want confrontation. Most would like to live in peace, have clean water to drink, and a future for their children. Many want to love and pray in a way that aligns with their truth. As we notice these commonalities, we become more accepting, understanding, and welcoming.

It all starts with walking through life with an open heart rather than a clenched fist. Being kind, compassionate, and loving is not a temporary state of mind. It is a way to move through life. A measure of who we are, and our connection with our true self.

To be xenodochial, is to be truly authentic. We cannot limit ourselves because of our false beliefs, negative self-talk, or unwarranted fears. The future of our world depends on how we learn to get along with those who appear different from us.

It all begins with understanding that at some point in time we will be foreigners. Our beliefs will differ from those around us. Our point of view may seem old-fashioned. But if we are living an honest life, someone will be welcoming and kind to us. Someone who has a xenodochial personality.

X-Factor

THROUGH MUCH OF SCHOOL MATHEMATICS WE are asked to solve for X. The equation may look something like this; if B is that, and C is this, then what is X? Once we arrive at X, we have the answer.

This is all well and good, until we realize <u>we</u> are "X." The person we are today is the totality of our life experiences, added to what we have learned from these experiences. The equation would look something like this; everything we have experienced, plus, everything we have ever learned, equals who we are at this very moment.

We are the X-factor. We get to choose how we react to challenges, roadblocks, or failures. Yet we also get to choose our behavior when we are successful, popular, famous, or wealthy. Our actions will reveal to us if we are authentic or living by our ego.

The interesting thing about solving for X in math, is the equation is never the same. Life is similar. We could go through two situations that appear exactly alike, yet the outcome will be different because of what is going on within us emotionally.

For example, yesterday my dog barked at the delivery driver. I didn't care, accepting that he was just protecting the house. Today my dog barked at the same driver, and I flipped out. The difference is the emotional state I was in at the time. I was the X-factor, I was the uncertainty in the situation.

Tomorrow the same delivery driver might show up, my dog will bark, and my reaction could be completely different. It all comes down to how I am feeling, and the challenges I have faced on that day.

Much of life is consistent. The sun rises, the sun sets. Tides come in, tides go out. We go to work, then we come home. How we react to everything in the course of our day will reveal to us if we are in control of our emotions, or just reacting to whatever comes along.

The way we go through life is up to us. If our emotional stability is inconsistent, then life will feel as if we are on a rollercoaster. One moment we are up, the next down, going left, then thrown right. Our emotional state of being is the variable, the X-factor.

All of us will face challenges throughout our lifetime. How we choose to handle these difficulties will alter the course of our life. We often think that life happens to us, in some cases this is true. Most of the time it is up to us to decide how we deal with these challenges. The choices we make will be the X-factor to our success.

If we accept that everything in life is out of our control, including our behavior, then we are the variable. Our actions determine the successes we will have, or the failures we will face.

It can be difficult to accept that we are the X-factor in our own life. We often blame everyone and everything when we fail. Yet we must be honest with ourselves when we look in the mirror to see how our behavior played a role in the final outcome.

Whether we choose to be responsible or not, it comes down to how courageous we are in accepting our part in how things turn out. Think of it this way, it's raining, we have a choice, wear a raincoat, or not. We know it's raining. We also know we will get wet if we don't wear a raincoat, but the X-factor is if we choose to wear a raincoat or not.

If we wear the coat we stay dry, if not, we get wet and we only have ourselves to blame. The formula is straight forward: raining plus wearing a raincoat equals staying dry. Simple enough. Look at it another way, raining plus not wearing a raincoat equals getting wet. Having the freedom to make our own decisions is the X-factor.

How we go through life is a choice. We can deny this powerful truth, thinking life happens to us, but when we realize we are the variable, the X-factor in the equation of our own life, we might be more conscious of the choices we make.

X-Ray

WHEN WE CONSIDER THE WORD "X-RAY" we commonly think of being in the emergency room having x-rays taken of a broken bone, or when the dentist x-rays our teeth. The purpose of an x-ray is to look beneath the surface to see if problems exist.

What if we were to compare an x-ray to our innate ability to see and feel emotions hidden below the surface? How often have we noticed someone in pain even though they haven't said a word? We can feel it, we know something isn't right, but on the surface there are no clues.

It's not only when a person is in pain that our x-ray "vision" will reveal the truth. Oftentimes we can feel if someone is not being honest or if they are hiding something from us. Our x-ray vision will pick up on their negative energy.

The thing about having x-ray vision is we know we have the capability to look beneath the surface, but for some reason we don't trust what we see or feel. There is also the possibility we don't want to know what is going on within another person because the truth may hurt us deeply.

To be the best version of who we are, we must learn to look beneath the surface to find the limiting thoughts and beliefs preventing us from living an authentic life. When we master this skill, we will have the ability to know who and what is best for us. But we must be strong enough to turn our x-ray vision on ourselves.

By looking within ourselves, we can uncover the hidden traumas festering beneath the surface. These painful experiences have the potential to keep us from living to the fullness of who we are.

It takes courage to use our x-ray vision. We may see things we don't want to see or admit. Once we recognize these traumas, whether in ourselves or others, we can bring them to light, where healing can begin.

As we allow light to shine on past negative experiences, we can tackle the root causes of the pain. This may not be easy, but the quality of our life depends on our ability to heal from our past suffering.

The intention of an x-ray is to see what needs to be healed within our physical body. We may not realize it, but many physical ailments have an emotional origin. When we begin to heal ourselves emotionally, many of our physical ailments begin to subside. It is important to recognize the connection between what is going on within us emotionally and our physical well-being.

Our desire to live an authentic life gives us the courage to look within ourselves to recognize what past experiences are limiting the way we walk through life. We must clear away the memories weighing us down. These memories have the power to block us from experiencing a true and meaningful life. They also have the potential to hinder our ability to know our own self-love, along with our ability to express our love to others.

Think of an emotional x-ray as the key that opens the door to a healthier way of life. As we look within ourselves, we may notice beliefs that hold us back from experiencing our self-love. Yet we must learn to view our x-ray without judgement.

This can be difficult because we may want to blame others for the way our life has turned out.

If what our x-ray vision shows us makes us uncomfortable, then these things need our attention. In the long run this negative energy is not healthy for us if we continue to keep these emotions suppressed. Their negativity can then become our underlying state of being, manifesting as physical illnesses.

As we become more comfortable using our x-ray vision to see what needs healing within us, we come closer to realizing our authentic self. It is in this place of authenticity we align with our inner truth. This will allow us to be true to ourselves, no matter how the world perceives us.

Y

Yearning

Have you ever had that feeling? A yearning to know the truth of who you are? A deep desire to uncover your authentic self? It can be a feeling that won't go away, no matter how often we journal, meditate, or walk in nature. This yearning comes from deep within us. It's not something we can satisfy in the physical world, yet we try.

A true yearning is difficult to explain to others, let alone ourselves. Yet this feeling keeps pushing us forward to dive deeper into our darkness, to reveal the light burning at the core of our being.

It can be an unsettling feeling because in the beginning we have no idea where it originates. We search the outer world for ways to quell our yearning, but nothing works. Only when we begin the journey to uncover the truth of who we are, do we realize our yearning is encouraging us to reconnect with our true self.

Imagine at the core of our being is an eternal source of unconditional love. This love is who we are, it is our authentic truth. When we align with our truth, we have arrived at a place of honesty, love, and stillness.

At some emotional level we know our authentic self exists, yet the challenges of the physical world have separated us from this awareness. We change who we are in many ways to please others, trying to fit in, hoping to boost our fragile ego. Yet our ego is not who we are. It is a persona we create, a coat of armor we think keeps us safe, but all it does is distance us from our true self.

Think of this yearning as the feeling of going home to meet our true self once again. Like an old friend we have not seen in years. We are drawn to them because they know us better than anyone we have ever met. When we meet, after so many years apart we realize we are looking into our own eyes, recognizing our own face, sensing our own heartbeat.

The yearning we feel but cannot explain, is a desire to know the truth of who we are, what we can accomplish, and to experience the self-love we have not felt for a very long time. Our yearning is our true self calling us back to a time when we were one being, working in unison to fulfill our destiny. A destiny to love ourselves and those around us without judgement, conditions, or expectations.

This calling may not be easy to answer. The physical world changes us. We walk off course thinking we are on track only to realize later we are unsure of who we are, uncertain where we are going, or can't understand why we are here in the first place.

To journey back to our authentic self, we must learn to shed many of the thoughts and beliefs limiting our ability to experience our self-love. Oftentimes the love we feel from the physical world is not love, but an attachment to those who share our same point of view. Although it may feel like love, it leaves us feeling hollow, yearning for something deeper, something with more meaning, something that endures the pain and suffering that often happens with attachments and conditions.

We may experiment with many things to fulfill our yearning: sex, drugs, alcohol, adrenaline, to name a few. Yet the yearning is still there. No matter how often we increase the dosage, the strength of the yearning never fades.

Eventually we crash emotionally because we convince ourselves we have tried everything to satisfy the yearning. Everything but quieting our mental chatter to hear the loving voice of our true self.

As with any journey into the unknown we may need a guide. Looking within ourselves, we notice our inner voice speaking its love for us. We realize this voice has always been there, leading us in the right direction, but for some reason we chose to ignore its guidance.

Now with our yearning growing in strength, our loving inner voice guides us through the maze of uncertainty and fear, taking us by the hand because it knows our yearning is an invitation to live an authentic life.

Our feeling of yearning is always there, tugging us in a direction we may not have considered. Yet knowing love is the destination, we can let go of our hesitation, and allow our yearning to lead the way.

Yes

THE WORD "YES" CAN BE A very powerful one if we know how to use it to our advantage. How often do we say yes to an obligation only to regret it later? Do we say yes so people will like us, fearing if we said no, they would not welcome us into their circle?

When we say yes for the purpose of boosting our stature with others, we are saying no to our authentic self. Our yes is a concession. We seek validation so we say yes, even though we know we are not being true to ourselves. Once we recognize this pattern, we understand the harm we cause ourselves when we say yes without consideration for our emotional well-being.

As we look over our past, we may notice times when we said yes, even though we knew we should have said no. Yet for some reason we continue this behavior knowing it may not be beneficial for our mental health. Is our hope that by saying yes we will find love and acceptance from those around us? Why is it we fail to realize that when we say yes to others, we are saying no to ourselves?

When we learn to say yes to ourselves we reconnect with the love found at the core of our being. By saying yes to the truth of who we are, we place our needs first. We take care of ourselves, thereby knowing what we need physically, emotionally, and spiritually. Once we align with these aspects of our truth, we can give to others without sacrificing any aspect of who we are. We then help others because we love helping those in need.

It may take time before we have a clear understanding of how saying yes to ourselves can change the direction of our life. Imagine yes as the key that opens the door to our full potential. We lock this door every time we say no to ourselves. Can we look at our behavior honestly and recognize the times we said yes to others, thereby blocking our way forward?

Saying yes to ourselves may not be easy at first. We may doubt our ability to stand up for ourselves when those around us question our choices. Or we may fear the unknown. Not having confidence in our ability to work through challenges may prevent us from walking through the door of possibilities.

It might be easy to change our mind if we feel too much pressure from the outside world. Our desire to be liked and accepted by others can influence how often we say yes or no. But how we feel after will reveal to us if we have made the correct choices or not.

With each new and powerful yes we say to the world, our self-confidence builds, increasing our inner strength, so when questioned we can stand by our decision. We then realize that at the foundation of this inner strength is an eternal source of self-love.

It is this love that gives us the courage to say yes to ourselves, even though it may mean no to others. When challenged by those around us, our self-love enables us to say yes to ourselves no matter what others think.

By saying yes to ourselves, we open our heart to receiving the gifts the universe has to offer. We place ourselves in a frame of mind that sees the possibilities that were once hidden from view.

Gaining the inner strength to say yes, when at one time we would have said no to ourselves, we begin to walk through life with our self-love as our guide. This love will never let us down and will always lead us in the right direction. It may take time to trust this love, because we have said no to it for many years.

As we begin the journey of reconnecting with our authentic self, saying yes to ourselves will be the light the guides us through challenging times. When we say yes to ourselves, we clear away the roadblocks that prevent us from living a life of unlimited potential. Yet it all begins with having the courage to say yes.

You

Look in the mirror, who do you see? You! You will not see those who doubted you. You won't see those who supported you either. Although supporters and doubters teach important lessons, you must learn these lessons yourself, then put these lessons into practice. The only person you see in the mirror is you, the one doing the work to live to the fullness of who you are.

This book has been written for you. The person seeking a better life through a connection with your authentic self. Congratulate yourself for doing something to improve the quality of your life. It is your life after all, no one can live it for you, nor do they know the dreams and goals you hold close to your heart.

At times life can be challenging, possibilities may not work out as we had planned, relationships change, opportunities seem to disappear. Yet when we are true to ourselves we move through these crises a little easier. Not unharmed, just a bit less damaged.

Through these difficulties you continue to work your way forward, trying to summon the courage to be the best you can, while maintaining your authentic self. Isn't that what life is about, being true to yourself when the world places unrealistic expectations on you?

Only you know what is true and worthwhile for you. Others

may suggest a path, yet the choice is ultimately yours. This is where life gets difficult. The people who claim to love you want you to go one way, yet you feel you would rather go your way.

Those who do not have the inner strength to remain true to themselves will move in a direction that pleases others, thereby denying themselves the opportunity to see what they are capable of accomplishing. Yet by living this way, at some point resentment and bitterness may begin to set in. In time this negative energy will be revealed in the form of anger or health issues.

Although we all want to please others, we must realize our happiness should be our main priority. This happiness runs deeper than just having a cocktail with friends. This level of happiness creates a foundation of truth and honesty, a foundation we need to build an authentic life.

When we are deeply happy, we are connected with the love at the core of our being. This love encourages us to explore the world to see what is available to us, then gives us the strength to grow from these experiences. A love such as this only asks us to be true to ourselves, without having to sacrifice ourselves for the pleasure of others.

We may seek the approval of those around us, yet we cannot stake our happiness on what they think of us. No person can keep others constantly happy. At some point our actions will be called into question, even criticized. If our happiness or identity is attached to the way others feel about us, we will surely be disappointed and let down emotionally.

Living an authentic life is finding the courage to love ourselves so we do not have to seek the approval of others as a measure of our self-worth. When we love ourselves, we no longer change who we are to make others happy. Nor will we urge them to change who they are to please us. Also, we will have no need to ask those close to us to live a life that does not bring them true joy and happiness.

There is a lot of responsibility being you. Your job is to walk a path no one else can understand or see. Yet that is where life becomes exciting and worthwhile. You have a mission few can comprehend. Yet those who do know, encourage you to move in a direction that resonates deeply within you.

You are as unique as the stars in the night sky. You have a choice to shine brightly or dim your shine to please others. The outcome will depend on the strength you have to connect with the truth at the core of your being. No one can walk this path but you.

Yūgen

Have you ever been so captivated by the beauty around you, you couldn't contain your emotions? The Japanese have a word for this, "Yūgen," a profound, mysterious sense of the beauty of the universe that triggers a deep emotional response.

Imagine being so in tune with our authentic truth, we experience a profound sense of beauty everywhere we look. When we align with the love at the core of our being, our eyes open to the beautiful mysteries of our world.

Oftentimes when we are searching for meaning, we come upon a place having deep emotional significance. We can't explain it, yet we know this feeling is more than a passing emotion.

To experience these kinds of emotions we must shed the limiting beliefs preventing us from seeing the whole picture clearly. When we look into the night sky, what do we see, a vast emptiness? Or do we marvel at the beauty, wondering what potential exists in those tiny white dots?

We often forget that the energy which created all we can see in the vastness of space, also created you and me. As we clear limiting beliefs from our consciousness, we realize we are one with the universe. Planets, distant suns, moons, the entire thing, are part of who we are. There is no separation. This kind of thought can overwhelm us, or it can cause us to experience a deep sense of connection.

It is our relationship to that which we cannot explain that allows us to realize how unique we are. No two grains of sand are exactly alike, nor are two people the same. Even identical twins are unique in their own way.

When we silence the mental chatter circulating in our head, we have the clarity to see the beauty in everything around us. This state of awareness allows us to know the truth of who we are, yet it also reveals to us a source of wisdom we cannot hear or understand if our mind is full of useless noise.

Think of a time when we experienced the feeling of connection with a source of energy outside of our physical body, something we knew to be greater than ourselves. We may have noticed it in a fleeting moment, a feeling we could not explain, but something we felt.

Did we shrug off this feeling? Or did we see it as a slightly open door? We did not know what was behind the door, but we felt drawn to it. As we stood before the door, we were uncertain what to expect, yet we remembered that feeling. Can we open the door to see what lies beyond?

Contemplating this kind of emotional response, the closest we can describe it, would be a powerful feeling of love. A love unlike anything we have ever experienced from the physical world.

When we silence our self-doubt, and the voices of our limiting beliefs, we allow ourselves to experience a stream of love so beautiful we cannot describe it. This love must be felt to be understood. Even then, the questions that arise will never be answered in a way that fully expresses the depth and magnitude of this love.

One of the challenges we face in attempting to explain the feeling of yūgen is trying to compare it to experiences in the physical world. This love is so beautiful, it can be difficult to explain. Although we quickly learn to trust this love because it only asks us to return to our true selves and then to love ourselves unconditionally.

Any persona we have created to protect ourselves is a shield preventing us from experiencing the pureness of this love. The façade we build, thinking this is who we are, limits our ability to feel the beauty of this love. Yet when we begin the journey to rediscover the truth of who we are, we stand naked before this love. We have no reason to hide, no need for the emotional armor we once used to protect us.

This eternal source of love is nurturing and kind, beautiful in its purity. Yet for some reason, we do not realize that this love is to be found within us. The depth of this love goes beyond any love we may have experienced in the past. A feeling once felt, never to be forgotten. To remind ourselves of this love we look to the night sky, reconnecting with the loving energy of all creation.

The beauty of this love wants us to be true to ourselves. Then and only then, will we begin to feel this love filling our being. This is yūgen, a profound, mysterious sense of the beauty of the universe that triggers a deep sense of love.

Z

Zen

Have you ever been in a situation where everything flowed easily? Your mind was calm, your mood peaceful, and you were keenly aware of what was going on around you? It's hard to explain, but it felt as if you were in a state of Zen.

The Zen state can be mysterious, it may not happen to us often, although when it does, we feel different. It's as if we are one with our surroundings, connected to a source of energy greater than ourselves, thereby elevating our consciousness.

When we enter an awareness of Zen, the noise of the world is silenced. In this state of being, our senses are enhanced. We may smell the fragrance of a blooming flower, feel a gentle breeze across our skin, we may even hear the beating of our own heart. Zen is a place of stillness, heightening our awareness.

Zen offers us the clarity to recognize our connection with everything around us: trees, animals, other humans, as well as the stars and planets visible in the night sky. A deep awareness of this connection can only be experienced when we are in a Zen frame of mind.

In a powerful state of Zen, we accept ourselves as part of the bigger picture. We are not separate individuals, we are one being, working together to live in harmony. Zen allows us to see the commonalities we have with others, as well as the responsibilities we have for the planet we inhabit.

Being in Zen gives us the opportunity to understand that love unites us as one people. There are no differences between us because of skin color, gender, national borders, or language. We are a community living on a blue planet floating in the middle of space.

Oftentimes the beliefs we were taught as children created walls separating us from anything that did not look or sound like us. These beliefs, no matter how well intended they may have been, prevented us from knowing our authentic self, yet they also limited our ability to accept others for who they are.

When we begin the inner work of releasing false beliefs from our consciousness, we step closer to realizing the truth of who we are. One way to do this is through meditation. It is here we come face to face with the limitations that have shaped our lives.

As we sift through the thoughts and beliefs preventing us from being authentic, we gain insights into who we are meant to be. This allows us to detach ourselves from many of the needs we have. A powerful need that requires our constant attention is our need for the approval of others to boost our self-worth.

We often change who we are as a means of pleasing others, thereby stepping away from our authenticity. The more we uncover our true self, the deeper we move into a state of Zen.

Through our inner journey, we begin to hear the voice of our higher self. We know this voice to be true and real by the love it has for us. The guidance we receive from our higher self is founded on an eternal source of unconditional love.

Becoming more aware of this love brings us closer to an awareness of Zen. Imagine walking through life guided by this never-ending flow of love. Negativity no longer bothers us because all we feel is love. We stop asking the outside world to fulfill our needs because our self-love reinforces our self-image.

Zen becomes our new state of being as we think, speak, and act through love. We have no need to judge or criticize ourselves or others. We understand everyone is doing the best they can at this moment in time.

Where we place our attention affects our awareness because Zen can only be reached in the present moment. That is one reason meditation is so powerful. We silence our mental chatter by focusing on the present moment. This allows our self-love to flow through our consciousness.

With practice we can arrive in a Zen state anytime we sit quietly in meditation. Yet it is not only in meditation when we can achieve Zen. When we are true to ourselves, living an honest and meaningful life, aligned with our authentic truth, Zen will come naturally.

There is no need to search the outside world for Zen, it is a part of who we are. All we must do is connect with our eternal flow of self-love. It is here we will discover the stillness and peacefulness of Zen.

Zenosyne

REMEMBER AS A CHILD WHEN SUMMER vacations seemed to last forever, and the school year felt like there was no end in sight? Then as we got older, time began to fly by. Why is that? Is it because with more responsibility time accelerates? There is a word for this, "zenosyne" the sense that time keeps going faster.

As we grew in age, summers became shorter, family holidays went by in a flash. Was it because we became aware of time? As young children, time didn't exist. We were told when to get out of bed, when to eat, and when to go to school. All this changed when we learned to tell time.

Could it be we feel time is moving faster because we are always rushing? Off early to work, rushing to the gym or market, hurrying to pick the kids up from school. Rushing to appointments, rushing, rushing, rushing. Never feeling as if we have enough time because we have so many obligations. Our days get shorter, we sleep fewer hours because we have overbooked our schedule.

It is possible to slow zenosyne? What would happen if we took an honest look at our life to see if we can apply the brakes? Not with the intention of stopping time completely but trying to back off our frantic pace. In doing so we might have more time.

One thing we must realize is our time here on Earth is

finite, meaning at some unknown point our life will come to an end. As depressing as this may sound, the quality of our life will be determined by how much time we had with those we love, and if we found time for ourselves.

There is little we can do about the spinning of the clock. What we can do is evaluate what is truly important, then move in that direction. This will give us the ability to feel connected with the world around us. If we are always in a hurry, we may miss a once in a lifetime opportunity.

One way to slow the feeling of zenosyne, is to pursue a passion. Many artists talk about being in the studio for what seemed like minutes only to realize it was hours. This is the effect of being in the zone. The focus is so intense, time does not exist.

Another way to ease the pace of life is to ignore the distractions that bombard us every day. How often do we look at our phone to see if there is a new email or scroll social media to check out the latest trends? Nothing burns time quite like endless doom scrolling.

Our phones can be wonderful tools, yet they can also be the reason we feel so rushed. We feel bad about ourselves because we read a post about getting out of bed at an early hour so we can do this or that.

Although this may be great advice, we are too exhausted from the day before to even contemplate getting up earlier. Feeling rushed and believing we don't have enough time can create a certain level of anxiety thereby causing us to sleep poorly. We have not cleared our mind before bed, so we try to fall asleep thinking of all the tasks we did not accomplish.

Yet zenosyne is a state of mind. Our belief that time is moving faster is something we tell ourselves. The mind can be a useful tool when we want to change our beliefs. If we convince ourselves we don't have enough time, then we have created a mindset based on this belief. On the other hand, when we believe we have plenty of time, we have the power to slow the pace.

The heart is the driving force of our life. If we are in a rush, we notice our heart beating faster. By slowing our heart rate, we have the potential to slow our pace. But it all comes down to becoming aware of how we feel in relation to what we are doing.

We are stronger than we will ever know. As long as we focus on how little time we have, we will always have the feeling of zenosyne. Yet when we focus on our ability to be true to ourselves, time will adjust to our way of thinking.

Zest

Have you ever noticed the most successful people are the ones with a zest for life? No matter how difficult the journey, or heavy the load, they greet each day with a positive attitude. It is their zest for life that carries them over any obstacle, whether physical or emotional.

For some, this zest is easily available, they are ready to jump in and give their all. Yet for others, there is little zest in their life. Why the difference? One reason could be the ability to overcome challenges. If a roadblock seems too great, many give up, admitting defeat while those with a zest for life view obstacles as opportunities for learning and growth.

Each of us will face difficulties throughout the course of life. The way we handle these situations will indicate how resilient we are. When we feel defeated, our zest for life will lead us toward a positive outcome. It will all depend on whether we have the inner strength to keep moving toward our dreams.

Our circle of friends can influence our zest for life. If we associate with those who have no ambition, we may not have the motivation to break free from our comfort zone. We want to be liked by others so badly we often remain in place rather than having to find new friends.

Yet when we have a zest for life, we surround ourselves with others who are comfortable with our desire for success. Those who also have a zest for life encourage each other, support one another, even telling us what we may not want to hear.

Each new day brings with it opportunities to recognize the truth of who we are. We can fall into the trap of repeating old, unhealthy behavioral patterns, thereby limiting our zest for life. To live to the fullness of who we are, we must take an honest look at our behavior to notice those patterns hindering our ability to live a truly meaningful life.

When we have a zest for life, we are not afraid to shed the thoughts and beliefs no longer serving our well-being. We look into the mirror of our consciousness to see what is reflected back to us. Do we see blame, resentment, judgement, or a desire for revenge? Or do we see clear, positive thoughts based on love, kindness, and compassion? What we see in our mirror will tell us if we have a zest for life, and if we are taking responsibility for our circumstances.

Once we are responsible for our actions, we free ourselves from the need to ask others to take care of us. We accept why we act as we do and take full responsibility for the outcome of our actions. Yet we must be honest with ourselves when we self-reflect, otherwise we will never move past our limiting behavior.

The thing about having a zest for life is we are comfortable with who we are, although we are not stuck in an unhealthy identity. We are unafraid to try new things, think new ideas, even contemplate a different course of action. We realize new ways of seeing the world will be found in questioning our point of view.

A zest for life is having the clarity to see opportunities few can see, then knowing what to do with this information. This is the exciting part of having a zest for life. We take action even though we may not be able to see the next step. We have learned to trust ourselves and know the right guidance will come to us at the right time.

Having a zest for life is knowing rain will come, but understanding flowers need moisture to bloom. We are grateful when it rains, yet we rejoice when the flowers reveal their beauty.

A zest for life is a state of mind we can strengthen by seeing the silver lining on a cloudy day, appreciating the lessons challenging situations have to offer us. Knowing that no matter how hard we fall, we will be lifted by the eternal source of love found deep within our being.

Zest for life is realizing we can choose how we look at the world. From this attitude we create the life we are living. When we take a closer look, we notice the energy of our zest for life is proportional to the depth of our self-love. The deeper we love ourselves, the more energetic our zest for life.

Zone

Nothing feels better than being in the zone. Everything seems to flow. Answers come easily, solutions appear out of thin air, all while we have endless energy. Being in the zone is a great place to be. Then there will be times when no matter how hard we try, we can't get back to that place of clarity. Those days are frustrating.

What makes the feeling of being in the zone so special? We are not talking about our comfort zone, that zone is a minefield of limitations. The zone we are discussing here is the feeling we experience when we are in alignment with our true self.

Each of us has a purpose in this lifetime. We may not recognize it because we have been taught to sacrifice our dreams for the benefit of those around us. This forces us to turn away from what brings us true joy, thereby denying ourselves the inner peace and wisdom we experience while in the zone.

There is no separation between the truth of who we are and what we are meant to do here on Earth when we are in the zone. We are one with our authentic self. Our life begins when we discover what is true and right for us.

A surefire way to know if we are in alignment with our true self is to notice how quickly we fall into the zone. Do our distractions and frustrations fade away? Are we experiencing an overwhelming sense of inner peace when involved in an activity that makes us happy? How we feel when doing anything will reveal to us if we are on the right path to living a fulfilling life.

The world offers us many great opportunities, we can be or do anything we set out to accomplish. Yet that can also be a challenge as we must find what lights our inner fire. This is where we learn to trust our intuition when moving through life.

If what we are doing makes us unhappy, we may not find the zone. Although discovering what brings us true happiness may be difficult, we will know our life has meaning as long as we are in alignment with our inner truth.

The thing about being in the zone is we can't fake it. No amount of coercion can get us into this elevated state of consciousness. It happens when we are fully present and connected with our higher self. It is the wisdom of our true self that delivers the right guidance at the right time.

Being in the zone unlocks our ability to receive wisdom we may be blocking during other times of the day. This guidance is always flowing to us, yet we only hear it when our mental chatter is silenced.

While in the zone, time seems to stand still, and we get much accomplished with little effort. We often ask why we can't feel this way throughout the rest of our day? One reason could be that when we are in the zone we are emotionally balanced, giving us the strength to ignore our distractions. When we step out of the zone, distractions and responsibilities flood our consciousness.

How can we stay in the zone? Meditation helps silence the noise in our head, giving us the opportunity to hear the guidance of our true self. This voice will comfort us when life becomes challenging. Yet this voice will also lead us toward a life connected with our authentic self. The more we follow this inner guidance, the closer we get to living in our zone every day.

As the world changes, our life may change as well. What once brought us emotional rewards may move us in a different direction. If shifts in life do occur, we may become frustrated because the inner peace we once found in the zone is no longer there.

When this happens it means life is offering us new possibilities to grow, and different avenues to discover what truly makes our heart sing. We will know what is true and right for us by how deeply we fall into the zone. It is in this place of clarity we reconnect with the truth of who we are.

Author Reflection

As I REVIEW THIS BOOK ONE more time, I reflect on how each subject could be a book in itself. I know I have only scratched the surface, but that was my intention. It's up to you to write your own alphabet.

Every one of us will have a different reaction to each "mini chapter." We will take away something different based on our experiences. When I reread certain chapters, different things resonated within me. What I once thought would be the main point, was overshadowed by something else. Although I think that's the burden of a writer. Nothing is ever perfect; we constantly find room for improvement.

Life is much the same way, it's rarely perfect, we can always tweak it just a bit. In a way, that's what makes this whole thing worth living, learning to adjust and change for the better, no matter how uncomfortable it makes us feel. Isn't that what it's all about? Shedding what no longer serves us, so we can return to our true self?

We have a responsibility to ourselves to write our own alphabet, our own narrative. This is how we move away from a life limited by our false beliefs to a world overflowing with possibilities.

That's the challenge, isn't it? To create our own story, a life of freedom to be who we truly are, without making excuses, or having to explain ourselves to those who do not understand.

The great thing is we have an alphabet. A series of letters that can help us express ourselves. When we learn to use the power of these letters, we can create a life we once thought was out of reach.

Peace and well-being,

Paul

Acknowledgments

I<small>T'S</small> <small>NOT EASY TO NARROW DOWN</small> the individuals who helped me become the person I am today. I should thank a middle school teacher who told me I had a defeatist attitude. Although painful to hear, it was the guidance I needed at the time. I still use her words as a source of encouragement to become a better version of myself.

I would like to thank my longtime friend and graphic designer, Elisa Tanaka, for her inspiring work on the cover as well as the design details throughout this book. I'm always impressed how Elisa can transform a title into a cover that represents the essence of the book. How she does it is a mystery to me. Thank you, Elisa.

I must acknowledge Mary Dado. Mary is more than an editor. I have become a better writer because of what I have learned from her edits. Yet I also feel Mary is a close friend. I reveal to Mary a side of myself few know, the vulnerable, unsure author, who hopes his sentences make sense. Mary's sensitivity to my writing gives me a level of strength and confidence I can trust. Thank you so very much Mary.

It's always a blessing when I meet people who understand me for who I am. Tracey Kern is one of those people. Throughout my career as an author, Tracey has been there guiding and inspiring me, while accepting me with all my quirks. Our bi-weekly phone calls help me remain centered and focused on the task at hand. Tracey has never let me slide and has always put the bar just a bit higher than I could reach. Thank you, Tracey.

Every day I wake up next to my wife Jane, is a day I cherish. No one ever told me a life partner would be so supportive. When I fall off track, Jane sets me upright, brushes off a bit of dirt, and helps me on my way. My writing would not be what it is today without the wisdom Jane shares with me. Being a writer can be scary. I often ask myself if anyone will read my latest article or post. Jane reassures me that if I had the inspiration to write it, then someone needs to read it. For this kind of loving companionship, I am forever grateful.

Finally, I want to acknowledge you, the reader, for joining me along this journey from Abundance to Zen. It takes courage to step into the unknown, away from the familiar with the intention of living a fulfilling life. I appreciate your determination to see who you are, what you can accomplish, and how deeply you can love. Thank you for encouraging me to write what is true to my heart.

About the Author

Author, blogger, and columnist, Paul Hudon lives with his wife, Jane, in the high grasslands of Southern Arizona where he finds inspiration for his books and articles. When not writing, Paul can be found exploring the diverse landscape with Jane and their dogs, mountain biking, or riding his motorcycle.

Also by the author

Your Inner Guidance, The Path to Discovering Your True Happiness
Published in 2021

A Complete Life, Discovering Your Authentic Self
Published in 2022

For more information, or if you would like to contact Paul, visit his website at:
PaulHudonAuthor.com

Made in the USA
Las Vegas, NV
22 July 2024